TWIN
SANITY

a how-to guide for
new and expectant mothers of twins

Susanna Pippel

ISBN-13: 978-1537153087

ISBN-10: 1537153080

•Contents•

Introduction   7

1. First Things First   11

>   *Answering initial questions about twins*
>   *and twin pregnancy*

2. Getting Ready Part I: the Intangibles   19

>   *Seeking information and help*

3. Getting Ready Part II: the Stuff   27

4. Maternity Clothes   53

5. Bed rest, labor, delivery, & the possibility of preemies   59

6. "You're breastfeeding twins?!"   79

7. "I don't know how you do it!"   95

>   *The daily routine*

8. And they're off!   117

>   *Solid foods, going out, and changes with growing babies*

9. This & That   129

>   *Babies and dogs, traveling with little ones, potty*
>   *training, big kid beds, adjusting to mommyhood*

Afterword   139

Acknowledgements   141

About the Author   143

Appendix   145

>   *Charts for keeping track, recommended resources,*
>   *recipes to make ahead and freeze*

Index   159

•Introduction•

Congratulations! I assume that if you're reading this, you are either expecting twins or you have a pair of beautiful new babies in your midst. Excited? Scared? Shocked? Overwhelmed? Overjoyed? Consider yourself officially part of the club.

When my husband and I found out we were expecting twins, our range of emotions at least doubled—or maybe squared. When we believed we were expecting one baby, we were excited and felt prepared—or at least as prepared as any first-time parents-to-be feel; when we learned that twins were on the way, we went into stunned panic. Suddenly, there was so much more to think about, so many issues to consider that are not on the table when you're expecting one baby, and so many unanswered questions. And, as we would soon find out, there were so few resources available. We did find a couple of books that seemed good—we liked them for their medical information, illustrations of what was happening in a twin pregnancy, explanations of certain terms that only expectant parents of twins need to know (such as twin-to-twin transfusion syndrome), and basic answers to questions like "Can the babies sleep in the same crib?" ...if you count wishy-washy yeses that are sure to mention that the American Academy of Pediatrics does not recommend it. What we could not find were books, magazines, or even quality websites with clear, step-by-step information about how we would survive each day managing to care for two babies at the same time.

When our girls were about ten months old, our pediatrician called, wanting to know if he could share my contact information with someone he knew who was expecting twins—her fourth and fifth children, bless her heart! She had asked him if he knew of any books or resources to help her prepare for having twins, and while he said he didn't know of any books, he did know of a person who would be a good resource if I would be willing to talk with her. Of course I was happy to visit with her, share the few books I did have, and encourage her. She had a huge advantage over me when I was pregnant—she at least was already a great parent. But I couldn't help thinking again, "This is ridiculous! There should be more out there to help new parents of twins!" That is when I started considering writing this book. There are countless books, magazines, and websites out there that address the concerns of new parents of singletons, but we need more to address the specific concerns of new parents of twins, especially since the number of twin pregnancies seems to be on the rise.[1]

It was several months after deciding that I'd like to write something to try to help soon-to-be parents of twins, and had not yet written a single word, that I had an epiphany—there are so few books out there about having twins because no parent of twins has time to write such a thing. And by the time you start to have some time, you have forgotten all of the critical details of the first few months with twins that would be so helpful for other new parents. So with five minutes here and five minutes there, I determined to put pencil to paper—or, actually, fingers to keyboard—to record everything I could remember about our journey through the first year with our girls. If not to publish for others, it would be a journal for my own memory and for our girls to read someday. (Like on a day when they're teenagers and complain about *me* waking *them* up when *they'd* rather sleep. Ha.)

Throughout the book, you will see passages in *italics*—these are excerpts from the journal that I kept when I was pregnant. My hope is that it will be of comfort to you to see how I was feeling and what

[1] J.A. Martin, B.E. Hamilton, S.J. Ventura, et al. "Births: Final Data for 2009," *National Vital Statistics Reports* 60, no. 1 (Hyattsville, MD: National Center for Health Statistics, 2011).

I was thinking at various stages. In addition to my personal opinions on what works well when caring for twins and ideas from other moms of multiples, you will find references to research, books, and useful websites throughout the book. For your convenience, these are also listed together in an appendix at the end.

This book is not meant to be the only resource you use, nor is it meant to replace the advice of competent medical professionals; this book is meant to be from one mom to another, full of real-life tips to help you survive and thrive during your first year with twins. I hope that you will consult a variety of books, magazines, and websites, and I encourage you to seek the advice of other moms who have twins. Take from each of us what will work for you and your family. And regularly and frequently check with your obstetrician, perinatal specialist, and/or pediatrician—they are the experts on all of the medical stuff. This book is simply what worked for this mom, and my hope is that reading this will help you feel more prepared for what lies ahead and provide some direction as you navigate through the first year with your twins.

•1•

First Things First

Before diving into too many details, I hope to address a few of the first questions and concerns you may be dealing with if you just found out you're expecting twins.

How did this happen?!

In our stunned brains, our first question was "How did this happen?!" Neither of us really has twins in the family, nor did we use any type of fertility treatment—in short, we were not at ALL expecting the doctor to hit us with the news that we were expecting TWO babies at our first OB appointment. We knew that fraternal twins occur when more than one egg gets fertilized, and that identical twins occur when one fertilized egg splits. But why did this happen with us?

Here's what I learned in my frantic online search after the blood had returned to my extremities:

Fraternal twins run in families. There is a genetic predisposition to ovulate more than one egg at a time, and either a mother can pass this trait on to her daughter (the mother, herself, having also had the predisposition to kick out more than one egg at a time), or a father can pass this trait onto his daughter (obviously not being an ovulator himself, but having this trait run on his side of the family).

Identical twins are "just a fluke." Or at least this is what I read over and over again. I like what my friend, Mary, told me: God makes identical twins when He sees a face that He really likes. But what about all of those families that have multiple pairs of identical twins in them? It seems that perhaps identicals also run in families, but that science just hasn't yet figured out why. (That, or maybe God really likes the faces in those families.)

You can expect to have people ask you if twins run in your family about once a day for the rest of forever. I tend to answer truthfully, but sometimes I think it would be easier to just say, "Yes," smile, and go about my grocery shopping.

What does 'high risk' mean?

Your doctor is the best source of information on this one. In short, it means that they're going to keep an extra-close eye on you to make sure you and your babies are healthy, and to make sure your babies stay inside you for as long as possible. Twin pregnancies are more likely to have complications, and twins are more likely to be born early, hence the "high risk" label. You will likely have more doctors' appointments and more ultrasounds than any of your friends who've had singletons, and you may also be referred to a perinatal specialist who specializes in high risk pregnancies and multiple births.

The great news is that medicine has come a long way, and while tragedies do still happen, there's a great deal that doctors can do to prevent problems and treat them if they do occur. If you do not feel that your doctor is competent in handling your high-risk pregnancy, I urge you to shop around if you can. Our obstetrician, Dr. K., was awesome, and we thought he was even more awesome for also sending us to a perinatal specialist, just to be on the safe side. Take the "high risk" thing seriously and do whatever is within your power to keep you and your babies healthy, but trust God to take care of you, too, and try not to lose too much sleep over it.

Am I going to need extra help?!

Well, it would be nice to have some extra hands around, but you can manage without extra help, too. Read on—more about this in chapters 2 and 7.

Oh my gosh—are we going to need TWO of everything?!

Some things yes, other things no. Read on—more about this in chapter 3.

What if I mix them up?!

You probably won't. You'll probably just be able to tell them apart... eventually. One of our daughters has a slightly rounder face than the other, they developed some "birth" marks several months after they were born, and their voices sound just a little different. And they definitely have their own personalities, although they do tend to switch temperaments from time to time—one will be particularly sweet for several days or weeks while the other is acting spicy, and then they'll switch. We even thought we had figured out that one was right-handed and the other left-handed, but they switched that when they were younger, too, before eventually settling into being a righty and a lefty. You probably won't mix them up, though. But I did paint one of Caroline's toenails before removing their hospital bracelets, just in case.

I was planning to breastfeed—can I still nurse TWO babies?!

Yes! Read on—more about this in chapter 6.

Will I ever sleep again?!

Yes! Read on—more about this in chapter 7.

How BIG am I going to get?!

Pretty big, but you'll laugh about it later. Read on—more about this in chapter 4.

As our first OB appointment neared, I was getting anxious to see our little one on the ultrasound machine and hear Dr. K. tell us that everything was going fine. At 11 weeks, I was certainly feeling pregnant—I'd been nauseous all the time until about a week before and had succumbed to lengthy daily naps, as growing a baby apparently takes a lot out of you! And even though no one else could tell yet, Stephen and I could see my belly beginning to grow and I could definitely feel my pants getting snugger by the day.

We went to the doctor on Wednesday, and after visiting with the nurse, Dr. K. came in and started talking with us about our pregnancy in general. He flipped through my chart, and pointed out my hCG (human chorionic gonadotropin) hormone level from the last blood they drew about three weeks ago. I knew from talking to our friend, who is a physician's assistant in town, that the hCG level increases exponentially during the first trimester and should have been somewhere around 40,000-50,000 when I went in for blood work three weeks before. The number Dr. K. pointed to was 139,000. Hmmm... He sort-of chuckled as he said, "Your numbers here are extremely high—you know, this could mean you're having twins!" Stephen and I looked at each other, looked at him, and I said, "You know, that's not funny." I think I even said something like, "Welcome to the doctor's office; here's your heart attack!" Dr. K. said, "I'm not really joking. It could be. We'll take a look in a minute here and see."

Moments later, Dr. K. revved up the ultrasound machine, had me lying on my back, and placed the magic ultrasound wand against my belly. It didn't take an MD to recognize that there were TWO little craniums in there. "Well, guess what guys," Dr. K. said. "Is that what I think it is?" I asked. "Yep—looks like you're having twins!" Stephen moved closer to me and held my hand as the doctor moved the wand around some more, getting a better look at our babIES. We laughed to ourselves in shock and disbelief as the doctor described what we were seeing on the screen. Tears welled up in my eyes. Two?! We saw two babies next to each other with a thin membrane between them. This was good, we were told, because that means there's no chance of them getting tangled in each other's umbilical cords. Was there any way to tell if they were identical or fraternal? Not unless we can see in a few weeks that one's a boy and the other's a girl. Otherwise we'll just have to wait until after they're born! And the thin membrane between them isn't so thick that it suggests that they're fraternal, but since it's there at all we can't assume they're identical either. Dr. K. moved the wand to one side so we could get a better, more up-close look at each baby. He measured Baby A—just the right size for a baby this far along. We could see him/her moving around, kicking its legs, and we could see its little heart beating rapidly—about 175 beats per minute. Then Dr. K. moved the wand to the other side so we could see Baby B. Also just the size he/she should be at this stage, also kicking and moving around, also with a strong heartbeat—about 155 beats per minute.

Wow. Just seeing such images on an ultrasound would have been mind-blowing enough. But twins?! Two babies?! After getting snapshots of each baby and the two together, ultrasound time was over. Stephen gave me a kiss. Dr. K. flipped the lights back on, and we talked about a few things before the end of our appointment time. Now there were other things to think about—for example, now that we were talking multiple births, we were talking about a high-risk pregnancy. We needed to start thinking about whether or not we wanted to plan on a c-section, since unless both babies are head-down for delivery, an emergency c-section could be required anyway. Would the babies make it to 40 weeks? Almost definitely not—apparently if multiples make it to 37 weeks, the doctors call it good and go in after them, so our babies would probably be born around December 7 instead of closer to their due date of December 29. Hmmm... Oh, yeah, I knew I had some questions written down—thank goodness I'd written them down—there was no way I could think clearly enough to remember anything at this moment. Among other items on my list was my friend, Katie's, wedding date of November 17. I had already told my dear friend, Jennifer, that I wouldn't be able to fly to her Philadelphia wedding in November, but I'd been wondering if I might be able to drive home for Katie's wedding, even if I were too big to fit into a bridesmaid's dress. I simply said, "Well, I guess I won't be traveling for any weddings in November," and crossed that item off my list.

Dr. K. congratulated us and shook our hands, and on the way out of the examining room, Stephen held up two fingers at the office staff. "It's twins!" They were all very excited for us. We walked down the hall to the lab so I could have some blood drawn, and while I was waiting, Stephen called work, telling them they'd better take him off the flying schedule for the rest of the day [the only time before or since that he'd ever done this] *because he was in no shape* to fly—he just found out we're having twins! (His friend/flight-commander good-naturedly laughed at him on the phone.) We left the office probably looking like deer in headlights. What exciting news! What completely shocking news. We kept looking at each other. Two babies? Two babies?! Two?! Huh…

We kept returning to this first ultrasound picture, which we had put on our refrigerator, to make sure we hadn't hallucinated the whole thing.

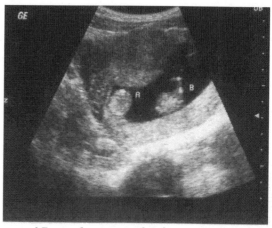

On Thursday, as the initial shock was wearing off, I began to feel a little bit panicky. Okay, so now we had to think about a scheduled c-section, and two babies at 37 weeks instead of one baby at 40 weeks. What if the babies came even earlier than that? What if I have to go on bed rest for weeks? I'm going to need maternity clothes much sooner than I thought. Now we need two cribs, two car seats, two high chairs, two names! two of everything. We'll probably need something bigger than our Honda Civic sooner than later— probably something bigger than the 4-door hatchbacks or small SUV's we'd been considering. For the past several weeks, I'd been going through life happy-go-lucky, thinking, "This is cool. I'm pregnant! I'm not worried about pregnancy, or even labor. I'm not worried about us having a baby to take care of." Now, I had much more to think about! And all the pregnancy books I owned combined only had about 10 pages in them about twins. I had some studying to do. And the phone kept ringing all day, with people calling to congratulate us, often after saying, "Is it true?!" That kept my spirits up, but I was feeling pretty anxious about it all. I just kept telling myself, "We can do this. God has never given us more than we can handle. It'll be fine. It'll be wonderful. We can do this."

After another night's (restless) sleep, I woke up Friday feeling much better. That was yesterday. Today has been good, too. Stephen and I went to the bookstore last night and found a good book about twins, and it's good to read some and become more knowledgeable about all that's happening now and will happen in the not-so-distant future.

Last Sunday, our Director of Christian Education, Debbie, delivered the sermon—her final sermon, since she had to leave our church to attend to some medical issues with her parents. The sermon title was "Surprises." The gist was that you can either camp out in worry, or trust that God will take care of you. What a timely message! This has definitely been the biggest surprise/shock of my life, but I'm not going to worry about it. I will plan, yes, but I will try not to worry—God will take care of us! - June 16, 2007 (12 Weeks)

•2•

Getting Ready Part I: The Intangibles

Seeking Information and Help

Multiples Clubs

What a great idea these are! They're often called Jonesville Parents of Multiples or Smith County Moms of Twins—something like that—and you can find them by searching Facebook, the Internet, or asking around in your city or town. You can also look for twins clubs at the Multiples of America (formerly known as The National Organization of Mothers of Twins Clubs) website, http://www.multiplesofamerica.org/ (although not all clubs are affiliated with the national organization). If a club exists in your city or town, I highly encourage you to look into it—they'll probably let you sit in on a meeting before joining, and it'll probably do you a world of good to talk to other parents of multiples. Plugging into a club's Facebook page, where you can easily ask questions and quickly get answers is also a fabulous resource—although nothing beats actually spending time in the company of others who understand what you're going through. When my girls were four, another mom-of-twins friend, Ellengray, and I formed a group in our town. It's amazing to see the instant camaraderie that happens when you put a group of women together who share the bond of raising (or expecting) twins. These clubs also routinely put on consignment sales, which are excellent places to shop for clothing and gear.

When our girls were coming along, we lived in a town without a multiples club. If you do not live in an area with its own multiples club, try to find a mom or two who has twins and chat them up. Most people love to give advice and are happy to share what they've learned. (Just look at me writing this book.) I was feeling pretty panicky until I met a friend of a friend who had a toddler plus ten-month-old twins. She invited me over for lunch one day, and it gave me *great* peace of mind to see that she was calm and her life was under control. All three of her daughters were happy and thriving, and she was glad to answer any questions I had. That was literally the first day that I felt at peace after we learned that we were expecting twins.

Helping Hands

I read over and over when I was expecting that I had to have my mom come to stay with us for several weeks and/or we needed to hire a night nanny to get through the first few weeks with twins. I tried to be optimistic, but this really freaked me out from time to time, because A) We lived 900 miles away from our parents who were all still working/unable to come and stay with us for an extended period of time, and B) We simply could not afford to hire that kind of help. If you, too, have been freaked out by such assertions, take heart—you CAN do it without going to these measures.

I do, however, encourage you to take help when you can get it, as long as you keep two very important things in mind: 1) You only want help that will truly be helpful, and 2) People who add stress to your life are not the kind of people whose help you will need. For example, my grandmother, whom I adore, did not visit us when our girls were newborns because at 86 years old, no matter what her intentions, she would not have been a whole lot of help. Nor is this the time for your five-year-old niece to tag along with your sister because she wants to see the babies. If your aunt is going to expect you to cook for her and ask you to freshen her martini while you're up (for the 12th diaper change of the day), she is not invited. You will have enough to do and enough to adjust to without that kind of "help." Further, if your brother-in-law typically causes you a lot of stress, you don't need his "help," either. You may try to convince yourself that you'll need all the extra hands you can get, that having these types of people around would be good, but having two newborns and raging postpartum hormones is more than enough stress for anyone—do not add anything extra.

You will also want to be diligent about allowing only healthy visitors into your home—and kindly (but firmly) insisting that they wash their hands or hit the Germ-X the moment they enter the house. Those who truly care about you and your babies will not want to see them get sick (and will not want to see you have to care for two sick babies) and will be happy to oblige. Don't be afraid to let your inner "mama bear" come out if that's what it takes to protect your babies.

You need people around you who will make your life easier and your postpartum time happier, not harder. This is both in the interest of making happy memories of this time and in *protecting your health and that of your newborns*. Your body needs a peaceful home in which to recover, and stress can and will have adverse effects on your recovery and your ability to produce enough milk for your sweet babies. Hopefully you can find some tactful way of keeping unhelpful/stress-inducing people from setting up camp in your home, and if not, you can always blame those crazy pregnancy and postpartum hormones for making you something less than the charming hostess that you would normally be.

All of that said, when people who bring you joy offer to help, let them! And when they vaguely say, "Call me if you need anything..." tell them right then and there that you would love to have their help, and ask them to tell you right then and there when they can come over, and then write it down or plug it into your phone. If you're like I am (sometimes too independent for my own good), you'll hesitate to call and ask for help. That, or you'll be so busy and tired that you won't want to fool with picking up the phone, or you won't be able to remember who all the people were that made those offers to help.

> Ask a close friend to organize other friends who've offered to help.

Another idea is to enlist a trusted friend to contact people in your group—maybe people at church, from work, from a club, or who were at a baby shower—and line up help for you, especially for the first week or two that you're home. My angel-friend, Annette, did this for me, which is just one of the many amazing things she did for us. I had someone at my house from our Bible study group every morning the first week that the girls were home from the hospital—when my husband had had to go back to work after taking two weeks off after the girls' birth, and my family had already had to go back home—and it was a tremendous help. She told me who would be at my house on which days, and they just appeared as if from heaven, without my having to make a single phone call.

Sometimes it's hard to think of what you need when people show up at your house, so you might like to have an ongoing list of things to do that you can show a helper and ask them to choose something. I felt uncomfortable asking friends and acquaintances to vacuum my house, but it really did need to be done and I didn't have time to do it—and a lot of people don't mind doing that at all. Things like that were on my list, and some people came in and did one thing, others crossed off several things in one visit, and they were all delighted to feel that they had helped. (Or at least they did a stellar job of making me think so!)

> Have a running to-do list for friends who show up and ask what they can do to help.

Another fantastic friend asked people at a shower she co-hosted to sign up if they would like to provide a meal for us after the babies were born. We also had someone in my husband's squadron coordinate meals with that group. All I had to do was say when we could use dinner, and these fine folks would call volunteers who would then show up with food. Wow. I think we asked for meals on Mondays and Wednesdays, figuring we'd have some leftovers on the days in-between and would be better able to cook for ourselves over the weekends—we didn't have to really cook for WEEKS. I can't say enough about the grand difference it made to have delicious meals that we didn't have to cook ourselves! TakeThemAMeal.com is a great tool for organizing meals. Share this address with a close friend who can round up people to provide meals for your family after the babies are born. It even has a "Click here to order" link for people who want to send a meal to you without actually cooking anything. http://takethemameal.com/

Many people helped us tremendously in those first weeks. I have to tell you about my favorite helper, though, so that you might have an idea of the best help you can get. My angel-friend Annette, whom I mentioned earlier, was nothing short of amazing. In addition to being a wonderfully supportive friend before the girls were born and arranging for others to come to our aid, she would arrive ready to work. Yes, she wanted to love on our girls, but her first priority was to make *my* life easier. She came armed with muffins for breakfast, trays of sandwiches to last us for days, and her jogging shoes so she could take our dog for a run. She would change diapers if she happened to be holding a baby whose diaper needed changing, or if I left the room to feed a baby I'd come back to find her washing the breast pump paraphernalia that had piled up in the sink or folding the load of baby clothes that were sitting in the dryer, all while singing to the baby who wasn't being fed. Things just got done when Annette was around. I never had to ask her to do anything. She only made my life easier—much easier. When she left I could look around my house and feel that I could breathe, that I could rest (even if only for a few seconds) in the calm that she had brought to the chaos that goes with adjusting to life with a pair of newborns. Annette, I love you!

If you do have the means to hire extra help, feel free to take advantage of it. While we were far from rolling in cash, in hindsight, I do wish I'd found someone to clean our house for us every couple of weeks for the first few months of the girls' lives. It would have been a load off not to have had to worry about that. We did hire some housekeepers when our girls were about four months old and my husband had broken his ankle—I quickly found that for me, having one more person to care for who couldn't carry a baby, push a vacuum cleaner, or get his own water was my limit, and that we either needed to hire some help or accept living in a pigsty for the next six to eight weeks. We chose to hire some nice ladies, and the first time they cleaned our house, I almost cried. It was totally worth it.

Classes

Yes, we took the hospital class on "prepared childbirth." We had the option of either going once a week for several weeks or knocking it out in one Saturday, and we opted to do it all in one day. It was surprisingly beneficial, even having a C-section as I did—I was still in labor for quite a while before my C-section, and I was glad I knew how to breathe through the contractions. I also recall the instructor answering a lot of questions about the women's center at that particular hospital, what to expect from the nursing staff immediately following delivery, what happens if you need to have a C-section, etc.

I also took a class on infant care, which was offered at our Air Force base by the same lady who taught it at the hospital. I'm glad I took it, but I wouldn't say it was totally necessary. Someone else who's recently had babies could probably give you the same tips they'd give you there.

The Baby Signs class I took was interesting and made a lot of sense to me, but I didn't make a point of teaching it to the girls except for a couple of basic signs. You can get that info from a book.

And I took an infant CPR class a week before the girls were born—I was too big to get down on the floor and practice the steps, but they "certified" me anyway. ☺

Registering for Gifts

Some people are not comfortable with this concept and feel as if they're asking people to get stuff for them. The thing is, though, that people who love you want to give you things—you've probably given a baby gift or ten, yourself—and registering helps people choose things that you'll actually like and use. (As long as you only tell people where you're registered if *they* ask, you'll avoid coming across as if you're "asking for gifts.") Especially when you're expecting twins, there will come a point before the babies are born when "I'll just run out and exchange this gift for something else" becomes a daunting task. So register! You'll be glad you did. You can get started anytime and add or delete things as you go. A lot of places provide a username and password to access your registry online and add things from home.

> Ask a friend who's recently had a baby to help you register.

Tip for first-time parents: Ask a friend who's recently had a baby to go with you to register for gifts, especially if you're headed to a baby superstore. The first time my husband and I went in one of those places, I nearly had a panic attack. No exaggeration. There is an unbelievable amount of stuff in there, and it's hard to distinguish between what's really useful and what is manufactured for new parents who can be suckered into buying things they really don't need. We had no idea what to register for, and it would have been so helpful to have some good advice! (They often give you a printed guide at the store, but that was not nearly as helpful as a real, live mom would have been.)

And now...the stuff...

•3•

Getting Ready Part II: The Stuff

We might not have known exactly what to expect with twins, nor did we know exactly what we would need to take care of them, but one thing we did know: We did not want to wait until the last minute to get ready. For one thing, as we've already established, there's a lot more to think about when you're expecting multiples. For another, once the little bundles arrived we knew we'd be even busier than new parents are when "just one" comes along. AND we knew that when you're expecting two or more, you're much more likely to go into labor early, have your babies earlier than your due date, be on bed rest, or at the very least, be too big and uncomfortable to want to leave your couch to do anything more than go to the bathroom. So start planning/registering/shopping early. Better to need to return stuff later than to not have what you need when you've got two babies to take care of.

Here are some pointers on what you really need to do, what you really need to buy, what you might like to have, what you really don't need to spend money on, and what this mom's opinion is on certain "controversial" items.

Must-Haves

Diapers

If there is anything you will definitely need, it's diapers. I understand that cloth diapers have come a long way since we were babies, and if you feel like tackling that extra laundry, more power to you. Personally, I figured I didn't need one more chore to do and planned on using disposables. I was a little paranoid about buying too many diapers too soon, afraid I'd jinx us or something, but there came a point that I started buying a package of diapers or wipes or a Diaper Genie refill every time I was at the grocery store, and boy was I glad I did. For one thing, it reduced the shock to our budget once the girls arrived. For another, it was a relief knowing that there was no danger of running out when we hadn't slept in forever and could barely remember to eat, much less to check to see if we had an adequate supply of diapers. Additionally, it was a huge help when my friend, Melanie, who co-hosted a baby shower for us, encouraged guests to bring a package of diapers for a prize. We had lots of diapers by the time our girls were born, and it was awesome!

Diaper Sizes

I'd recommend picking up at least a couple of packages of preemie-size diapers. Many full-term singletons can fit into this size when they're newborns, so there's an excellent chance that your twins will be little enough to wear these. Keep them in their packages and hold on to the receipts, though, just in case you break a world record and have 40-week, ten-pound-each newborns.

In addition to preemie-size diapers, get several packages of newborn-size (N), and if you feel like it, buy an assortment of other sizes in the 1-3 range. Really, though, they'll probably wear newborn-size for a while and size 1's for quite a while after they're born.

I preferred for our babies to wear the smallest size diapers they could fit into, as the smallest ones are the least expensive—you'll notice as they grow into bigger diapers, the price of each package stays the same but the number of diapers decreases (i.e. the cost per diaper goes up). Plus, they are less prone to leaking when they fit a little more snugly.

How many diapers will they use?

I had many friends with singletons who would give me diapers that they had leftover from when their babies outgrew a size mid-pack. This would crack me up (as I graciously thanked them) because we went through so many diapers there's no way we'd outgrow a size before we could use up the rest of the package.

> Plan on 8-10 diapers per baby per day.

How many diapers did we use? You'll need to change them with almost every feeding, and maybe even a little more often than that, so plan on 8-10 diapers per baby per day. We figured out pretty quickly that they would do just fine without a fresh diaper every time they tinkled, especially if we were diligent about putting Vaseline on their tushies at every diaper change. (In our experience, Vaseline was much cheaper and *more effective* than any diaper rash cream. There was even a nurse somewhere along the way who told us that the Desitin-type creams can adhere to baby's skin in a way that causes irritation when it gets wiped off. We did discover, though, that our girls seemed to be allergic to the baby-scented kind, but did great with plain old, regular Vaseline.)

A diaper per feeding is a pretty good rule of thumb. As you reduce the number of feedings per day and start to introduce solid foods (around 4-6 months at the advice of your pediatrician), you'll probably drop down to only needing 5-6 diapers per baby per day.

> Vaseline is an excellent diaper rash preventative.

Which diaper brand is best?

I encourage you to try lots of brands, because what works well for one baby may not work as well for another. We found that Pampers Baby Dry worked the best for our girls; I've heard lots of friends with boys say that Huggies worked best for them. Pampers were a bit more expensive than some others that we liked pretty well, too, so we'd use Pampers at night and our second-favorite during the day. Also, if the expensive ones seem to be the only ones that will keep leaks at bay early on, you might try the cheaper ones again after a few months—they may work just fine when your babies get older, are spending more time sitting than lying down, are eating a different

> Try different diaper brands at different stages of your babies' development.

diet, etc. You may also encounter an allergic reaction to one brand of diapers versus another—if one or both babies has a rash around the elastic area of the diaper, you might try switching brands.

Wipes

Go for the "sensitive" variety, free of dyes, perfumes, etc. Baby skin is super-sensitive, and you don't need mysterious rashes due to allergic reactions to add to your list of things to handle. You may search online for homemade wipes if you're feeling crafty and have a little extra time to make your own. You may also try tearing/cutting wipes in half to get a little more mileage out of each package.

Diaper Pails

I've known people to go without a special diaper pail, but we found the Playtex Diaper Genie II (in 2007) to be well-worth its $30-ish purchase price and $6-ish refills. The original version of the contraption used a sheath of plastic and a twisty device to create sausage-like links of diapers; the 2007 version was just one long bag in a somewhat stink-proof container that clamps tightly shut after each deposit. The volume of diapers you'll go through will probably still necessitate emptying it every couple of days, but a specially-designed diaper pail *does* make a huge difference in keeping your nursery from smelling like, well, you know…

Gear

Car Seats

These are a must-have if you intend to take your babies home from the hospital. My then 86-year-old grandmother said to me, "You won't need those for a while! You can just hold them in the car until they're bigger!" I hated to tell her that doing so would not only be extremely dangerous, but is also illegal, and most hospitals will not let you leave with a newborn until they've checked to see that you have an appropriate car seat that has been properly installed. Hospitals typically have at least one staff member who is certified to make sure that infants are strapped into their seats safely and that their car seats are correctly installed in vehicles. Many baby superstores, police stations, and fire departments also offer a safety seat checks. Go to www.seatcheck.org to find a location near you.

To each his own, but here's how we decided which kind to get:

A friend who used to work for the highway patrol told us that convertible infant-toddler seats aren't as safe as infant seats. Another thing is that most of the convertible infant-toddler seats won't hold children for as long as they need to be in some sort of booster seat, so you end up spending a bunch of money on a convertible infant-toddler seat, and then you have to go and buy another toddler-booster seat after that. We bought infant seats that fit newborns to 30 lbs. (Graco Safe Seats) in the hope that we could go straight from infant seats to bigger toddler-booster seats—and it worked. After the girls reached their first birthday and exceeded 20 lbs., we purchased toddler/booster seats (Graco Nautilus) that are rated up to 100 lbs. They'll probably use those till high school.

You might want to check out Car Seats for the Littles—it's an organization staffed by nationally certified Child Passenger Safety Technicians whose mission is to share injury prevention information with the public. They provide thorough reviews of child safety seats, from ease of installation to fit for children of various ages and sizes. Their website also includes a handy tool for comparing different car seat makes and models. http://csftl.org/

Many standard infant seats were designed to only hold up to 20 lbs. because *the old standard* was that it was safe for babies to face forward at 1 year *and* 20 lbs. We opted for the higher weight limit so we could keep them in the safer, backward-facing position for as long as possible. Now the American Academy of Pediatrics says that you should keep your babies rear-facing until they are two years old[2],

---

[2] O'Keefe. "New advice: Rear-facing car seats safer for children until they are 2," *AAP News* 30, 12 (Elk Grove Village, IL: American Academy of Pediatrics, 2009).

and the National Highway Traffic Safety Administration (NHTSA) recommends keeping them rear-facing up to age three.[3] As a reference point when trying to decide which seats to buy, the average two-year-old weighs about 28 lbs. The average three-year-old weighs about 32 lbs. The average four-year-old weighs around 36 lbs., and the average five-year-old weighs about 40 lbs.[4] Check your state laws to see what the current standards and regulations are for child safety seats where you live.

Strollers

While we're on the subject, you want a stroller that can hold the infant car seat carriers—you don't necessarily have to buy a matching set; many strollers will accommodate many different brands of infant seats. It's really handy to not have to un-strap and re-strap your little ones when you're out running errands—just unclick the whole seats, pop them in the stroller, and go. You see people carrying those infant seats around, but you'll quickly find out that you'd rather push a stroller—a 10-15 lb. seat plus a baby can get heavy. Even if you're burly and don't mind the weight, those carriers are really cumbersome and awkward to carry around—especially when you try carrying two at a time. Just make sure your stroller will hold TWO infant carriers, as many double strollers are designed for one infant and one toddler for all of those inefficient people who have their babies one at a time.

Tandem-style (front-to-back) strollers are great for getting in-and-out of doors when you're shopping or running other errands and are the style you're most likely to find when looking for strollers that hold car seat carriers. Snap-N-Go makes one that's just a frame for car seat carriers—very lightweight. Just make sure that if you order one, you find one that fits both the *make* and *model* of your car seats.

Side-by-side strollers are also nice to have. Some friends who have older twins passed one of these on to us, and we really enjoyed

[3] http://www.safercar.gov/parents/Right-Seat-Age-And-Size-Recommendations.htm

[4] Palande, Leena. http://www.buzzle.com/articles/average-weight-for-children-by-age.html, January 2012.

it when we were out for walks in the neighborhood so both girls could be "in front." They are not as practical, though, for maneuvering in and out of doors and through stores when shopping.

I am not a runner, but jogging strollers with their big wheels are easiest to push outdoors. They are pricier, but worth considering if you plan to spend a lot of time outside. We did not have one and enjoyed plenty of walks without one, but sometimes I wished we did.

One more stroller tip: Occasionally grease the wheels with a little WD-40 or silicon spray. One of our strollers was getting really hard to push, but my husband thought to lube-it-up, and it helped a lot!

Furniture

Crib(s)

To start, you need one crib. Our girls slept together until they were about eight months old, when they became really mobile and would try to play with each other in bed. The party line, however, is that it is not safe for twins to co-sleep, for fear that they will be a suffocation hazard to each other and increase their risk of SIDS. The threat of SIDS scared me silly, and I do not want to downplay the risk, but your newborns probably won't be able to move on their own for many weeks. And we really treasured the fact that our girls could be with each other, just as they had been in the womb, and not have to sleep alone.

We swaddled each of them individually, laid them side-by-side, and (because it was wintertime) wrapped a blanket around them as one bundle—this is what the nurses did in the nursery after they took

the girls out of their incubators. (The only reason they were in separate incubators was that they kept pulling out each other's feeding tubes!)

This is purely anecdotal—and I would love to see some research done on this topic—but of my moms of twins friends, those whose babies slept together slept better than those whose babies slept apart. Sleeping side-by side, our girls kept each other company and kept each other warm. I only wish they could have slept together that way longer! Just use good sense and put them in separate cribs as soon as you see them moving around and possibly putting each other in danger.

Our girls slept together until they were about eight months old, when they got so big and wiggly that they started waking each other up. After that, we had two cribs in the same room, and now they are in two "big girl beds" in the same room. Their crying did not wake each other up—they were accustomed to that sound from day one—and they still rarely wake each other up. We intend to keep them in the same room for as long as possible. After all, if Mommy and Daddy share a room, then so can they!

> Our nursery nurses were fabulous swaddlers— ask at the hospital if you want tips on effectively wrapping up babies.

We weren't stuck on having matching cribs, especially since some friends had offered to give us their crib, and we figured we could find better ways to spend our money than on a brand-new crib we didn't need. My friend, Katie (whose children have beautifully-decorated bedrooms), and I were talking recently about how much effort we all put into making our babies' rooms as adorable as possible…and then hardly anyone ever sees them. As it turned out, the crib our friends gave us was the same finish as the one we bought. I guess if you really want identical cribs, you might want to buy them at the same time or at least try to find out from the manufacturer if they intend to discontinue your crib within the next several months. If you're stressed about making their room look Pinterest-perfect, though, I hope you can give yourself the grace to erase that from your to-do list.

As far as convertible crib-to-toddler-bed cribs are concerned, I wouldn't necessarily spend the extra money. The crib we bought is "convertible," but my husband easily removed the front rail off of the other one (not "convertible") to make it into a toddler bed, too. Take a look at the way the cribs are assembled, and you might find that you could do the same, as well. Also, lots of friends have taken their toddlers straight from the crib to the big bed, maybe with a bedrail or pillows on the floor, skipping the toddler bed thing altogether.

Changing Table—or not

We hated the thought of buying a piece of furniture that we'd only use for changing diapers, so instead of buying a changing table we just had a changing pad on top of a dresser. It came with hardware to attach it to a dresser top, and it worked great. (Be sure that you follow the manufacturer's directions, always keeping your babies' safety in mind.) We had a basket next to it with diapers and wipes and stuff, and anything else we needed we kept in a dresser drawer.

Rocking Chair

You're probably going to want a way to rock your sweet little ones from time to time, even if you don't use rocking as a way to get them to sleep every night (more on that later). Be sure to try out the rocker you buy, as what looks pretty in a catalog or online may bump and jolt and not be so soothing after all.

Portable Play Yards and/or Bassinets

We found a Pack-n-Play to be an invaluable asset, especially because we didn't want our newborns lying on the floor within reach of our dog, Sugar's, very affectionate tongue until they had been around long enough for us to train the dog to keep a safe distance. We had two Pack-n-Plays—one was given to us as a shower gift, and the other was given to us as a gently-used hand-me-down. One we set up in our bedroom—the bassinet insert fit the whole Pack-n-Play, making a bassinet that was big enough to hold both of our girls. We rarely used it in there, though, because our girls' room was right across the hall from our room, so it was easy enough to hear them when they cried, and we found it difficult to sleep when they were in our room because of all the cute baby noises they made while sleeping. So glad we didn't buy bassinets!

The other Pack-n-Play we set up in our living room, which created a great place to lay a baby or two to play while there wasn't someone there to hold one or both of them. (Sometimes mommies need to have both of their hands free!) They loved it in there. And it had a bar to hang toys from, which gave them something to look at and play with once they got a little older.

They do make a Pack-n-Play with Twins Bassinet. As I said about cribs, I don't think it's really necessary to separate your teeny peanuts while sleeping, so the twins bassinet part doesn't particularly turn me on. The best thing about the Pack-n-Play for with Twins Bassinet is that it is larger than the standard version, but it's also about twice as expensive. You might prefer the bigger model if you intend to travel and have your babies sleep in there together when they're more than a few months old, but then you may still find yourself wanting a second Pack-n-Play to travel with when they get too squirmy and playful to sleep together. As for playing together in the play yard, a standard size is sufficient for two babies to play in. Whether you prefer one style or the other, I highly recommend having at least one.

Infant Seats/Bouncy Seats/Swings

If you are having twins, you pretty much cannot live without at least one of these. Really you need two. While I was nursing one baby, I would sit the other one in the Papasan Chair, bouncy seat, or swing. (And sometimes pick up a paci with my toes and put it back in the not-being-fed baby's mouth. But I digress.) Baby seats and swings are cozy, provide a great vantage point for looking around, and if you have a baby with reflux—or just one who tends to spit up more if he or she lies down too soon after eating—they allow Baby to sit up enough to digest food comfortably. Much like the Pack-n-Play, you need a place to set your babies from time to time—or a lot of the time—and having a couple of these items are perfect. Plus, when they reach 4-6 months and you start introducing "solid" foods (runny baby cereal), these seats are perfect places to feed babies who can't yet sit up in a high chair.

> When getting ready for bath time, take a bouncy seat into the bathroom with you so you have somewhere to put the baby who isn't being bathed.

I liked having two different seats, plus the swing, so the girls weren't sitting in the same things all the time. You may have babies who love the swing, so you might want two. The Papasan Cradle Swing moves both side-to-side and front-to-back and is generally amazing—I think it's well-worth the premium price.

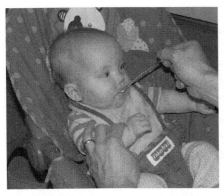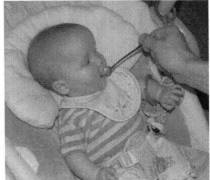

Abigail and Caroline, eating their first "solids" in a Fisher-Price rocking seat and a Fisher-Price Papasan seat

Clothing

It's so hard to know what you'll need to dress your little ones in! And it doesn't help that you don't really know how big they'll be or how fast they'll grow.

First and foremost, think practical. Indulge in a couple of adorable little outfits if you must, but remember that babies spend most of their time sleeping for the first few months of their lives. Comfort is key. And they will inevitably spit up and have the occasional leaky diaper, so you want things that are machine washable for sure. Also, newborns have difficulty regulating their body temperatures and can get cold or overheat easily, so layers are a good idea most any time of year.

I would definitely start with some onesies (shirts that snap at the crotch), both in long- and short-sleeves (obviously stocking up on more of one kind or the other depending on the time of year/climate when your babies arrive). The little "sleep and play" coverall outfits are also wonderful, easy, comfortable, and can be slept in or worn going out. You'll need some socks, and a lot of people swear by those newborn mittens to prevent them from scratching themselves, although we didn't use them. And hats—you'll need some of those little knit hats (knit like a t-shirt, not knit like your cool sister-in-law's knitting). I was disappointed in those sweet little infant nightgowns—they don't put drawstrings at the bottoms of them anymore (choking hazard, I guess), so they ride-up like crazy—I wouldn't recommend getting any of those.

As far as how many of each thing you need, you want to have enough to avoid doing emergency loads of laundry, but realize that you'll probably do a load of baby laundry about once every day or two anyway (you won't want to let spit-up on, peed-on clothes sit for too long), so you don't need a gazillion of each thing. Do anticipate multiple clothing changes each day, though, as those spit-ups and leaky diapers do happen. In selecting quantities, plan on a full set of newborn sized clothing on up—I would only purchase a few preemie-sized things, just in case. (Suggested quantities are in the list in the following pages.)

> Choose clothing sizes according to your due date, not the date you think your babies might actually be born.

Choose clothing sizes according to your due date, not the date you think your babies might actually be born. In other words, if your due date is at the end of December (as mine was) but your babies are born in mid-November (as mine were), you'll still need to plan on them wearing a size 3M about 3 months after your due date. (They'll likely be in preemie clothes until the time they should have been newborns, and then they'll start wearing newborn-sized clothes around your due date, and so on.) Also be sure to match the size with the season—it's amazing how many people don't think about that when they purchase adorable sleeveless 12M sundresses... for babies who will be that size in December. We were so sad for our girls to never wear some of the precious things that sweet people gave us, because the size and season didn't match up.

You can look forward to their growth slowing down a little in the second year, and once they reach a size 2T, their growth will slow down a lot and they'll wear toddler sizes for almost a whole year! Then buying clothing won't involve quite so much math.

Miscellaneous Items

Laundry

You may find yourself with ever-so-slightly more laundry to do than you had before... Be sure to get Dreft or some other laundry detergent for sensitive skin, and wash everything before wearing/using for the first time. I'd also highly recommend Zout stain remover (red bottle, in the grocery store with the laundry detergent). Chock full of enzymes, this is the best for getting out spit up and everything else under the sun. (A lot of the time, you'll wash things and they'll *look* clean, but if you store outgrown clothes and get them out to hand down to someone, spit up stains will reappear as if by magic—Zout may prevent that, and I've heard it'll even remove stains that reappear after storage.)

We kept bibs on our girls almost all the time to reduce the frequency of clothing changes and laundry to do. The Velcro that's on most of them is junk—they try to make it soft and smooth for babies, but that means it doesn't actually hold very well. And yet it's rough enough to catch on everything in the laundry! If you can find some with snaps, those are the best.

> I love bibs. I adore bibs with snaps.

To protect your clothes, you'll want some burp cloths. Cloth diapers are great for this, and we also loved the Gerber Interlock burp cloths—they were super-absorbent, soft, and pretty.

Additionally, we kept a cloth diaper under their heads in their crib to reduce how often we had to change the crib sheets due to spit-up. Eventually, Caroline adopted those cloth diapers from the crib as her blankies! I've always been glad that she was so attached to something that could be easily replaced in a 10-pack.

Pacifiers

For one reason or another, some people never give their babies pacifiers. Some folks are worried about orthodontic issues down the road (which I've read are not cause for concern unless your child still sucks on something at age four[5]); others worry about "nipple confusion" (see the chapter on breastfeeding for more about that); others just don't want to deal with having to break the habit later. At a recent mothers of twins club meeting, we were talking about how most of us had given our twins pacifiers, if for no other reason than to have another trick up our sleeves in the event that one or both babies started crying in public—I tried tricks A, B, and C, and now I'm trying a paci. If that's not reason enough, recent research suggests that taking a pacifier may actually help reduce the risk of SIDS and that sucking on a paci may provide pain relief.[6] (Think of all those immunizations!)

I used a pacifier when I was a baby (well, actually, I'm told I used three at a time), and I think I turned out well enough, so I didn't hesitate to allow my babies to use them, too. Some babies really take to pacifiers, and others don't. Both my girls liked them for a while, but then Abigail went to her thumb (as we saw her doing on one of our ultrasounds), and Caroline slept with a paci till she was (I'm a little embarrassed to admit) three. When they need a little extra comfort, a paci or thumb can be a God-send.

They'll probably give you some pacifiers at the hospital. You might also buy two newborn size pacifiers of one brand and two of

---

[5] American Family Physician http://www.aafp.org/afp/2009/0415/p681.html

[6] American Family Physician http://www.aafp.org/afp/2009/0415/p681.html

another, since it's hard to know what your babies will prefer. You can stock-up on a favorite later.

For more information on to paci or not to paci, go to mayoclinic.org and search for "pacifier use." The referenced article from American Family Physicians also provides excellent research-based information about the pros and cons of pacifier use.

Sick Baby Kit

I wish babies never got sick, but they do from time to time. They'll probably give you a bulb nasal aspirator at the hospital. You'll want to have one around in case you have a poor baby with a stuffy nose. My sister-in-law bought a contraption called a NoseFrida, which looks bizarre, but supposedly works great—it's basically a tube, one end of which goes in the baby's nostril while the other end goes in Mom's mouth to suck the snot out. (Sounds gross, right? You don't actually get snot in your mouth, though.) I'm not sure that my niece hated it any less than my girls hated the bulb aspirator. If they get a cold, though, you've got to do what you've got to do.

You'll also want a good thermometer on hand. Anything you find on the market is probably accurate enough to let you know if your baby's temp is roughly 98 degrees, 101 degrees, or 104 degrees, and whether it's going up or going down. We really like our digital model by Braun that quickly and painlessly takes readings in their ears.

Ask your pediatrician for a list of medications to keep on hand for emergencies. You don't want to call your doctor at 2 a.m., have him recommend a dose of a fever-reducer, and then have to figure out how to get to Walgreens in the middle of the night with two babies while your husband is out of town—it'll happen every time!

Most importantly, **do not hesitate to call your doctor**. If your baby is less than three months old and starts running a fever, your pediatrician will most likely want you to bring him or her in right away—or go to the emergency room—just to err on the side of caution. If you're worried about your child at any age, call the

> Call the doctor right away if your baby starts running a fever—generally considered 100.4 degrees or higher.

doctor—you will quickly learn to recognize when "something isn't right" with your child. Listen to that mother's intuition—you have it for a reason!

On a couple of controversial items:

Crib Bumpers

You'll read that crib bumpers are not recommended and increase the risk of SIDS. I have a friend who had such big custom-made crib bumpers that her toddler barely had room to sleep! And one time, before they lowered the mattress, her little girl fell out of the crib, probably because those bumpers were so thick that she could use them as steps to climb out. I believe that these are the type of bumpers that they warn against for fear of SIDS. As I've said, I do not want to discourage you from taking every precaution when it comes to your babies' safety, but that said, here's what we did:

We had crib bumpers by Carter's that were relatively thin. Ours were thin enough that if the girls stepped on them, they just flattened, and they did not take up any space in the crib to speak of. We had the bumper up when the girls were newborns and were too little to move around, then took it down when they started scootching but weren't (in my mind) strong enough to unpin themselves if they pushed their faces against it (for fear of SIDS). Then we put it back up when they were bigger and stronger. I found that (once they were more than about six months old) they would fall asleep more easily if they couldn't see out of the crib when lying down, and I could more easily peek in on them unnoticed with the bumpers in place. Without the bumpers, they would sometimes get their legs and arms stuck through the slats. Caroline took a pacifier for a long time, and without a bumper, pacis ended up everywhere but inside the crib. Still, when I would check on our girls before I went to bed at night, I would occasionally see one of them with her face up against the bumper, and in spite of the risk of waking her up, I'd move her out of fear that she'd suffocate. My husband thought I was paranoid and crazy.

Bottom line: the bumpers really aren't necessary, but they are good for some things, and they do look nice. I would go ahead and get one, and then use it when you feel it's safe and take it down when you don't.

Also along those lines, you really don't need a big crib blanket that matches the bedding/decor of your nursery, unless you just want to lay it in a chair or use it on the floor. You'll swaddle your little ones when they're little—maybe for many months because a lot of babies really like that—and it'll be much easier to keep them warm and cozy in a footie blanket-sleeper or sleep sack when they get too wiggly for swaddling. I was paranoid about using blankets with our girls (because of SIDS) until they were over a year old—and even then, they were small, lightweight blankets that I thought were "safe." I've even seen companies referring to blankets that match crib as "toddler blankets" now.

> For swaddling/receiving blankets, register for the waffle-weave thermal kind if you can find them. They tend to stretch a little and work better for swaddling than flannel ones. And the bigger, the better.

Electric Breast Pumps

Medela makes a fantastic double electric breast pump contraption, but the official word is that they are only intended for one user. They are only guaranteed for one user. You will read that there is an increased risk of infection if more than one user operates one of these. They will run you around $300, and if you are nursing twins, you really do need one of these. I have known very few women who have not worn themselves out (and caused themselves discomfort in the breasts and carpal tunnel syndrome in their wrists) trying to use a manual pump—and these are people who were only nursing one baby at a time. Your babies could very well come early, like mine did, and not be able to nurse for a few days or even weeks. (Our girls were born before their suck-swallow reflex had kicked-in.) If you want them to get breast milk (and I hope you do!) you may have to use a pump. Hospitals often have the "hospital grade" available to their patients, which you can then rent after you leave, often at the expense of your insurance company. My guess is that the biggest difference there is that a company like Medela can ensure that a hospital cleans the parts thoroughly, but they have no control over what individuals might do and thus tell individuals that they cannot re-use pumps.

My double electric breast pump had been used before—by two different mothers. I do not advocate buying one at a garage sale or from a stranger on the street, but the way these things work, it's only air that's being pumped through the machine itself. Mommy milk goes straight from the breast into a funnel into the bottle—all of which are dishwasher safe. My breast pump was originally purchased by my dear friend, Melanie, who then sold hers to another friend, who then sold it to me. I trust these women like sisters, and each time, the tubes (that only pump *air* from the pump to the funnel/bottle contraption, anyway) were boiled/bleached, and none of us had any problems. Or you could always purchase new accessories to go with your previously used pump. You be the judge.

Breastfeeding Paraphernalia

A few other items you'll need if you're nursing: nursing bras (see chapter 4), breast pads (Lansinoh makes great disposables), and Lanolin cream for nipples (I did better without, but some people swear by this stuff). If you're using a pump, you'll need breast milk storage bags—those made by Lansinoh or Medela were always of good quality. A Boppy or other nursing pillow is wonderful to have—they're also good for holding your baby, even if you aren't nursing. Search "twins nursing pillow" online to find one specially designed for nursing two babies at a time, if you intend to nurse simultaneously (more on this in the breastfeeding chapter). MyBrestFriend and the Twin Z Pillow are good nursing pillows, specially designed for moms of twins.

And they make some adorable nursing covers now for feeding babies when you're out-and-about, have company over, or just want to have something pretty to wear while you're feeding your babies at home in your old sweatpants and t-shirt. Search on Etsy for some cute nursing cover options.

Nice-to-Haves

Video Baby Monitors

The first time I saw one of these at a friend's house, I thought, "Oh, please. Isn't that a little over the top?" Once our girls began rolling over, sitting, and standing, however—and generally became more aware of people coming in to snoop on them—I could see the benefit of a video monitor. Often I'd wonder, "Is she crying just because she's cranky? Or is she stuck rolled over onto her tummy and can't get back on her back? Should I let her cry it out, or did she stand up and can't figure out how to lie back down? If I go in there, I could just disrupt her trying to settle herself down and then we'll be back at square one..." So I began to see why a video monitor would be nice to have.

When we moved after the girls' second birthday, we found ourselves purchasing a new monitor because our basic one did not work well in our new house. It picked up so much interference that we could hardly use it, but we really needed to have a monitor in our new home because the girls were upstairs while our bedroom was downstairs (first-world problems). A Levana video monitor was recommended because of its low interference, and we love it. I imagine it would have been great when the girls were babies, but it's also fun for the toddler/preschool years so you can see that your child is not sleeping, but is in fact jumping up and down in her crib and egging her sister on until she joins her. Or that your sweet girls are trying so hard to mind Mommy and not get out of their big girl beds that they keep one toe in bed while reaching to get a dropped, cherished stuffed animal—and quickly get right back in bed. We found a used one on eBay for about a third of the retail price.

People lived without monitors of any kind forever, but even in a relatively small house I still found it handy to have our basic model in our kitchen so that if I had the water running I could still see the lights flashing if someone was crying. Plus, it's nice to have a little freedom to roam to your garage or yard when your little ones are sleeping, keeping baby monitor in hand—with or without video.

Deep Freezer

One thought we had before our girls were born was that it sure would be great to have a bunch of meals cooked and in the freezer, food that we could just heat up on days that we didn't have time to cook—and we figured there would be many. Our freezer was always pretty packed as it was, so we invested in the least expensive chest freezer we could find (around $100) and put it in our garage, and it was one of the best investments we've ever made. A few months before my due date, we started making double recipes of whatever we were cooking, making big batches of soups and casseroles, and freezing them. It was wonderful! I've included some recipes in the appendix that are particularly yummy, filling, and freeze/reheat well.

Thank You Notes

It is my hope and prayer that you will receive a great deal of help in preparing for and adjusting to life with your newborns. We were tremendously blessed in that way, and it made our transition into double-new-parenthood so much easier. You'll want to thank all of those people who help you, so one last thing for your shopping list is a stack of note cards for writing thank you notes. And remember to pick up some stamps.

Must-Haves Right Away

Some moms may tell you that you don't really need an item or two on this list, but in this mom's opinion, these are items you won't want to live without:

Gear:

☐　　2 infant car seats

☐　　1 double stroller

☐　　1 or 2 bouncy seats/papasan chairs/swings

Nursery:

☐　　1 crib and crib mattress

☐　　2 crib sheets (per crib)

☐　　2 water-proof crib mattress pads (per crib)

☐　　6 swaddling blankets

☐　　Changing table pad and cover

☐　　Baby monitor (a must-have if you live in a sprawling space)

Clothing:

☐　　Diapers—preemie and newborn sizes

☐　　Vaseline (regular, unscented)

☐　　12 bibs

☐　　12 newborn onesies—short sleeve or long-sleeve depending

　　　on the season

- ☐ 12 0-3M onesies—short sleeve or long-sleeve depending on the season
- ☐ 6 newborn footed sleepers or "sleep and play" outfits
- ☐ 6 0-3M footed sleepers or "sleep and play" outfits
- ☐ 6 pairs of newborn socks
- ☐ 6 pairs of 0-3M socks
- ☐ 4 newborn baby knit hats
- ☐ 4 0-3M baby knit hats
- ☐ 4 pairs of newborn mittens to prevent scratching
- ☐ 2-4 of the above items in preemie sizes, just in case

Feeding:

- ☐ 24 burp cloths
- ☐ Double electric breast pump
- ☐ Breast pump storage bags
- ☐ 4 small bottles
- ☐ Breast pads
- ☐ Lanolin cream

Bathing & Grooming:

- ☐ 1 baby bathtub with newborn hammock
- ☐ 6 baby washcloths

- ☐ Baby wash

- ☐ 4 hooded baby towels

- ☐ 1 bottle baby lotion

- ☐ 1 box of baby cotton swabs

- ☐ 1 pair of baby fingernail clippers

- ☐ 1 super-soft baby hairbrush

Miscellaneous:

- ☐ Dreft or other laundry detergent for sensitive skin—wash everything before wearing/using

- ☐ Zout stain remover

- ☐ 2-4 newborn-size pacifiers

- ☐ 1 nasal aspirator

- ☐ 1 thermometer

- ☐ Thank you notes

Nice-to-Haves Right Away

- ☐ Rocking Chair

- ☐ 1 or 2 baby swings

- ☐ 1 or 2 Pack-n-Play portable play yards

- ☐ 1 Pack-n-Play crib sheet (per Pack-n-Play)

- ☐ Baby monitor (maybe a must-have if you live in a sprawling place)
- ☐ Small stereo for playing sleepy music at bedtime/naptime
- ☐ 1 nursing pillow with washable cover
- ☐ 1 nursing cover
- ☐ 1 crib toy/mobile per crib—we love the Fisher Price Ocean Wonders crib toys, which our girls still played with for years. They even make them with a remote control now—awesome.
- ☐ 1 or 2 baby carriers (2 if your husband wants to back-pack a baby, as well). The TwinGo is popular in my moms of twins group. http://twingocarrier.com/
- ☐ Deep freezer

Must-Haves Down the Road

- ☐ 2 high chairs (or 2 booster seats)
- ☐ 2-6 baby spoons
- ☐ 2 freezable teething rings
- ☐ Electrical outlet covers
- ☐ Cabinet door locks
- ☐ Baby gate, if you have stairs

Nice-to-Haves Down the Road

☐   2 shopping cart/high chair covers for grocery shopping and eating out

☐   2 Exersaucers or walkers

☐   2 Munchkin or other snack catchers for snacks on the go

Where to Shop

Before you look at this long list and start to feel overwhelmed, let me give you a few tips on where to procure these items without breaking the bank.

As mentioned before, eBay can be a great source for gently used items that are not safety-related. You don't want to buy used car seats unless you can be 100% confident in their safety records—car seats should be replaced after they have been in an accident—but there's no reason not to purchase a pricey baby monitor from a stranger, especially if that stranger is a highly-rated eBay seller.

Consignment stores specializing in children's wear and gear are also good places to find quality used merchandise, and weekend children's consignment sales have become a booming business. Duck-Duck-Goose, Just Between Friends, and Rhea Lana are a few of the big companies that host events all over the country. Many churches, moms groups, and multiples clubs also frequently hold sales. Search your city or state name and "children's consignment sale" online to find out when one of these mega sales is happening near you.

If you join a local multiples club, chances are that they have a Facebook page. Moms often post items that they're looking to sell (or give away) without having to prep for a garage sale or consignment sale. You can also post ISO (in search of)... if you're looking for something specific. Posting ISO among your Facebook friends can also yield results. Lots of us have stuff sitting around that we're more than happy to pass along if someone asks.

All of these are also good places to look for maternity wear. Which leads me to...

•4•

Maternity Clothes

I was so excited about the prospect of maternity clothes! I couldn't wait to wear things that made me look really pregnant. Although at the same time, I was worried early in my pregnancy that if I wore anything that even remotely resembled maternity clothing—at a time when trapeze tops and empire waists were hot—that people would think I was jumping the gun. I could not wait to genuinely need to wear maternity clothes and have it be obvious to the world that I was, indeed, pregnant.

That was before I found out I was expecting twins. After I found out that twins were on the way, I was still excited about my belly starting to "pop;" I just didn't have much time left to anticipate it.

I'm definitely showing now! We took a two-week trip to see family and friends, and by the end of our trip, there was no doubt that I'm pregnant. My sister, Allison, said, "It's like I can see you growing!"
-July 4, 2007 (15 weeks)

Before I knew it, my regular pants no longer fit, and I was wondering just how big I was going to get. What size maternity clothes do you buy when you know you're just going to get bigger and bigger *and bigger*? Should I bother buying a new bra now? I mean, my regular ones were too small, but just how busty was I going to get? And then there were nursing bras to consider. So many questions...so little room in my pants...

I bought some clothes here and there, and managed to keep my tummy covered (mostly). Here's what I wish I had done:

First purchase

A "belly band" or "tummy sleeve." This miraculous device is a big stretchy band that fits over your regular pants so you can wear them unbuttoned/unzipped. They sell them at Motherhood Maternity and Target, among other places, and they are a God-send for making your regular pants/jeans/skirts wearable and comfortable for longer. I wore one with a lot of maternity pants, too, when the elastic in them was not placed in a way that actually held my pants on. I also liked it as another layer over my bulging belly button when I got really big. You've gotta get a couple of those. I only wish I'd had one sooner.

Maternity clothing sizes

Most people wear the same size in maternity clothes that they wear in regular clothes; someone who normally wears a "medium" will wear a "medium" in maternity garb. Don't buy too far in advance, though. As an expectant mom of twins, chances are pretty good that by your third trimester, you'll outgrow the first size of maternity clothing and move up a size (or two). Shop as you go.

I'm not sure what I weigh right now, but we measured my waistline last Friday and it was 1 ½ inches more than it had been two weeks before. So I've now grown about 10 inches around, and at this rate, I could grow 10 inches more. Wow. Even my maternity smalls are getting too small—thankfully I've had a few friends loan maternity clothes to me, so I think I can hold out a few more weeks before buying anything new. The weather's getting ready to change, so I definitely don't want to spend any money on more summer maternity clothes. The good news, of course, is that this means that the babies are growing. I read today that they each measure about 8 ½ inches crown-to-rump, or 12 inches head-to-heel. So I have 24 inches of baby in me! No wonder strangers think I'm due any day now—one lady in Staples said the other day, "Oh...are you getting anxious?!" I suppose I could just say yes, but I feel compelled to be truthful and say, "Well, I guess, but I have a ways to go. They're twins and aren't due until December."

I'm feeling more comfortable with the idea of having twins now, although it's still sometimes overwhelming and hard to actually believe. A few days ago I was feeling really stressed because there's so much to do—and I feel like I'm playing catch-up from our having been out of town a couple of weeks ago, followed by being down for a week with a cold. And the closer we get to baby time, the less energy I actually have to do all the things we need to do. Then I was feeling frustrated a couple of nights ago because none of my clothes fit anymore. (In reality, I still have enough to wear—I was just having one of those girly moments where I felt like I had nothing to wear, compounded by pregnancy hormones.)

- September 7, 2007 (24 weeks)

Bras

I've always been an underwire kind-of gal, but I found them really uncomfortable as my bust grew with my pregnancy. Since I didn't want to spend a lot of money on bras that might not fit me for very long, I bought a bunch of inexpensive sports bras, and that generally did the trick (Hanes or Fruit-of-the-Loom at Wal-Mart or Target).

Nursing bras

They say that most women need a nursing bra that's one cup size larger than they'd normally wear, and that proved true for me—even nursing two babies at once. You'll want to go ahead and buy a couple before baby-time, but I would not recommend buying more than two or three at first—sometimes a style that feels comfortable in the store doesn't feel as comfy when nursing. You'll also want to stock up on disposable nursing pads. (Lanolin makes some great ones, available at Wal-Mart and Target in the baby department, and at baby superstores, among other places.) A comfortable sleep-style nursing bra should also be on your shopping list—yes, you'll want to sleep in some type of bra when you're nursing, if for no other purpose than to hold nursing pads in place.

While we're on the topic of what's going on with your changing body, I'll address this question:

Will I ever get my body back?

Yes…pretty-much…eventually…

A friend who recently had twins made it all the way to 37 weeks. At the end, her doctor told her she was measuring comparably to what a woman would measure if she were pregnant with a singleton…at 47 weeks. The best sound bite I can give you on this one is that it took about nine months to get your body so out of shape, and it'll take (at least) nine months to get it back.

My personal experience was that I shrank back down to my normal *size* pretty quickly—taking care of and nursing two babies (burning 500 calories per baby per day)—can do that to you. Within weeks I was back in my pre-pregnancy jeans, so you could say that I was back to my normal *size*, but I would not say I was back to my normal *shape*. Things shift when you're pregnant, and it takes a while for them to go back. I could wear most of my pants, but my tops looked bizarre—my tummy wasn't flat(ish) again for some time, and my bust continued to be much bigger than usual for as long as I nursed. (Okay, that part wasn't so bad.)

I found myself very frustrated a couple of months after the girls were born when I went shopping for something new to wear to a semi-formal party for my husband's squadron, and the things I pulled off the racks that normally would have looked cute on me all looked completely awful—I was just a different shape than I'd ever been before. (I did eventually find something to wear—in a style that I wouldn't have considered before and haven't worn since.)

Mothers of multiples are just as susceptible—maybe more so—to the stretch marks, varicose veins, and/or lasting belly button imperfections that many mothers experience. You may sail through without any of these, or, like me, you may consider having that umbilical hernia fixed someday. In the meantime, try to consider them battle scars of the unique, awesome experience you've had. I'd take my girls over the ability to wear a bikini any day. (Although it would be cool to be that woman who has twins *and* can wear a bikini…maybe someday…)

Probably the best advice I can give is as follows:

1. During pregnancy, eat right and engage in regular, low-impact exercise—according to the advice of your obstetrician.

2. Eat right after your babies are born. If you're nursing, this is extra important—if you subsist on a diet of chips and soft drinks, you won't be passing along the best nutrition to your babies. Eating well will benefit all of you.

3. You will naturally get a lot of exercise in the business of caring for two babies. Don't drive yourself crazy trying to get to the gym. Leisurely walks through your neighborhood will be good outings for your babies, will get some fresh air for all of you, and will get you some time out of the house. But if it's good for your mental health to go to the gym while Dad watches the kiddos, do it for the sake of "Mommy Time"—not in the quest for physical perfection.

4. Be patient. Go easy on yourself. Appreciate the miracle that has just happened through your body—something far more impressive and important than outer appearance.

The girls are VERY active now. They usually get kicking shortly after I wake up, and go through active periods after most meals and around 11:00 a.m. and 5:00 p.m. They were so busy moving and kicking and elbowing the other day that I found it hard to take a nap in the afternoon when I wanted to. It's not so much that they kept waking me up as it was that I find their movements so fascinating that I couldn't sleep for wanting to stay awake and feel them move! Usually I can't really tell which one's moving, but sometimes I'll feel a lot of movement back and forth on both sides of my tummy, and it's those times that I figure they're both moving around.
—September 7, 2007 (24 weeks)

•5•

Bed Rest, Labor, Delivery,

& the Possibility of Preemies

One of my main concerns when we found out we were expecting twins was how having twins would change labor and delivery, including the fact that labor and delivery could happen earlier than we had anticipated, and that we could have a pair of preemies to care for. And it was a bit daunting thinking of how it would feel to carry two babies—especially near the end.

I'm excited to be at 28 weeks today because this is the magical week when the survival rate for preemies jumps to 90%—what's even better, though, is that we still don't have any reason to think that the girls will be born early.

We went back to Dr. S. (our perinatal specialist) in Oklahoma City on September 18, and he said everything still looked good. At that time, the babies weighed 1 lb. 9 oz. and 1 lb. 13 oz. He said that a 4 oz. discrepancy is nothing to be concerned about, and that they may actually be closer to the same size, but it's impossible to get an exact reading. They both still had plenty of amniotic fluid, and he

> **Twin-to-Twin Transfusion Syndrome (TTTS)** is a rare condition that can occur in identical twin pregnancies. Normally, identical twins share the placenta without any problems, but in TTTS, the babies do not get equal blood flow. Untreated, this can lead to a variety of serious or even fatal conditions. Be sure to talk to your obstetrician about TTTS.

said we'd gotten to the point that if they start showing signs of twin-to-twin transfusion syndrome, they'll just monitor them closely and deliver them if necessary. It was a relief to hear that. My friend, Annette, said that she could tell "a cloud had lifted." Not that I was depressed or anything before, but she could tell I felt relieved after hearing that.

I'm still feeling pretty good, but getting bigger and more awkward all the time. My abs are pretty much useless, so once I'm lying down I feel like a beached whale—it's really difficult to roll over or sit up—and it's getting more and more difficult to get up from a sitting position, as well. We have a habit of sitting on the floor at the coffee table to eat dinner, but I've had to move us to the table like civilized people because it's really uncomfortable for me to get up off the floor—especially with a full stomach.

I'm also noticeably more tired again. It's a rare day that I don't take a nap...or two. Thankfully, I have an open enough schedule to do this, but it's still frustrating to accomplish so much less in a day than I would if I weren't pregnant—and to feel like there's so much more to do. I was freaking out about this last week when I'd had three simple errands to run on Friday, but was too tired to do all except one. Stephen settled me down, though, and we got a lot done over the weekend, which made me feel much better.

-October 5, 2007 (28 weeks)

You know how miserable women seem at 39-40 weeks when they are carrying "only one" baby? Let's just say I think that equating carrying twins late into the third trimester with what it would be like for a singleton mommy going to 47 weeks (like my friend who measured comparably to that at 37 weeks with twins) seems like a fair comparison. Uncomfortable is an understatement. But here's why it isn't so bad: Any time you're in a high-risk pregnancy, you're extra thankful for every day that your baby or babies stay inside you—the longer they stay put, the healthier they're likely to be. Also, the discomfort comes on so gradually that you don't notice it as much as you would if you just woke up one morning having swallowed a lead-filled beach ball. I really didn't notice how uncomfortable I had been feeling until *after* my girls were born, and I suddenly felt so much better. And finally, should you have to have a c-section, you'll still probably feel so much better after the babies are born that some soreness from major surgery doesn't seem like such a big deal.

Before getting into all of the labor and delivery stuff, let me say that I know twin mamas whose babies were born at around 37 weeks or so (considered "term" for twins), were delivered naturally, never needed to be in the NICU (neonatal intensive care unit), and had zero complications with their pregnancies, births, or newborns whatsoever. I don't know many of those, and I was not one of those, but it can and does happen.

Like all expectant mothers, I hope you'll have a birth plan for how you'd ideally like things to go, but even more so than for a mother of a singleton, I hope you'll be open to the idea that things may not go as planned—after all, twin pregnancies are considered "high risk" for a reason: You're more likely to have your babies come early, and you're twice as likely to have a baby be in a difficult-to-deliver position. Talk with your obstetrician ahead of time about your birth plan—and how reality may differ from how you hope things will go. Also review this plan with the nursing staff at the hospital, realizing that they deliver babies all the time, know how things are likely to actually go, and will always do what is in the best interest of you and your babies, which may or may not be according to that four-letter word, "plan."

It is especially important for expectant mothers in high risk pregnancies to be open to the idea that their deliveries may not go according to their ideal birth plans.

Premature labor

Most women experience Braxton Hicks contractions throughout their pregnancies—the contractions that usually go unnoticed, are irregular, infrequent, and are not associated with labor. If, however, you feel contractions occurring more than about four times an hour or are at all concerned for any reason, call your doctor.

> If you are concerned for any reason, call your doctor.

I think it was at around 24 weeks that I started feeling pretty frequent contractions—it's hard to say for sure, because for a while, I mistook the tightening of my uterus for one of the girls pushing her head into an uncomfortable position. Then, at about 28 weeks, I was having such frequent contractions that we wound up in the emergency room.

On Monday, October 8, I had to go to the hospital at about 1:00 a.m. with frequent contractions. Thank goodness I had Stephen at home to say, "Let's call the hospital and talk to one of the OB nurses," and "We should go ahead and call Dr. K;" Stephen could see that I was worried and was in quite a bit of discomfort and needed to go to the hospital, while I was trying to tough it out and not act on what I thought was maybe nothing. Once we got there, they hooked me up to fetal heart monitors and a contraction monitor, which indicated that the babies were doing just fine but that I was having contractions every 3-5 minutes—good thing we went in. They gave me a shot of Brethine, which stopped the contractions, and we were on our way home by about 3:00 a.m. Unfortunately, when I woke up at around 8:00 the next morning, the contractions started again, and we were back up at the hospital around 9:00. That time, I was having back pain with contractions every minute or so. They did a full urine sample and detected a urinary tract infection (weird, because I had zero symptoms of a UTI), which they suspected was causing the contractions—my body suddenly wasn't the healthiest place for the babies to be, so I had started working to get them out. They gave me two shots of Brethine this time and put me on an I.V. to make sure I was well-hydrated. At around noon I was sent home with antibiotics and instructions to do pretty much nothing until my appointment with Dr. K. on Wednesday.

I didn't stay in bed, but I sat in the LaZBoy with my feet up pretty much all the time until that Wednesday. Dr. K. was concerned about my experiencing preterm labor, but didn't see any need to put me on full bed rest at that time—although he said he reserved the right to change his mind in a week or two. He prescribed Procardia, a blood pressure medication that also acts as a smooth muscle relaxer to stop contractions. I can take it every 4-6 hours if I have to, but he only wants me to take it as needed when I have six or more contractions in an hour. So far, I've had to take it five or six times, and he's pleased that that's all I've had to do to keep the contractions at bay. Apparently, it's pretty normal with twins to have contractions like this for weeks before the babies are born. And I'm thankful that they're generally not painful—it's just really uncomfortable and a bit disconcerting to have your uterus tightening out of your control every few minutes for an hour or more at a time.

-November 1, 2007

Bed rest

Bed rest and multiple pregnancies are not necessarily synonymous, but there is an elevated chance that you'll be prescribed bed rest at some point in your pregnancy. Again, I know women who were never on bed rest of any kind while expecting twins; I also know women who were on bed rest for much of their twin pregnancies.

My experience involved little formal bed rest—only what is mentioned above, and my hospitalization for a few days prior to the girls' birth. I did, however, have to severely cut back my activities in the weeks following my initial episode with preterm labor. I found that even driving somewhere in our ten-minute, quiet town, would start contractions that I'd have to fight (often with medication) for the rest of the day.

Should you find yourself prescribed extensive bed rest, I hope you will let your fingers do some walking. There are many wonderful websites and blogs out there from women who are either in your shoes (or not allowed to wear shoes) or who have been there before. Sidelines National High Risk Pregnancy Support Network (www.sidelines.org) is a great place to start.

Labor

The good news as you read the next part is that this is about as bad as it gets. You may have a worse experience than I did, but that's pretty unlikely—a few mothers I know have had equally difficult labors and deliveries in one way or another—but most everyone I know had a much easier time of it than I did, and hopefully you will, too. I'll give you the unadulterated version in the spirit of honestly preparing you for what may lie ahead—but take heart that your experience may be much better than mine!

At about 31 weeks, the perinatal specialist (whom I was seeing every six weeks in addition to my OB) told me that I needed to start going to the hospital twice a week for non-stress tests. They would hook up the fetal heart monitors and a contraction monitor to make sure that all the contractions I was having were not distressing the babies. At that point, I was about to start seeing my OB once a week, the perinatal specialist every three weeks, and visiting the hospital twice a week—around three medical appointments per week.

By 33 ½ weeks, I was having contractions pretty much all the time.

When I went for a non-stress test last Thursday, I learned that I was having far more contractions than I realized and was told to start taking my Procardia every 4-6 hours regardless of whether I felt that I needed to or not. Yesterday at the non-stress test, I was having contractions every six minutes—even with the Procardia— but when the nurse called Dr. K., he said that as long as the babies weren't being stressed by it, it was fine. And, thankfully, the babies were responding just fine so I guess we won't worry about it. And I have pretty much felt like I've been having constant menstrual cramps for a week now—as long as I take my prescription super-Tylenol, it's not too bad, but as one would imagine, I'm getting pretty tired of not feeling well and am ready to start feeling good again. It's amazing how as you feel worse and worse in your pregnancy, the more ready you feel to care for a newborn (or two)! Oh—and Dr. K. told us last week that he and Dr. S. [my perinatal specialist] have decided that we need to shoot for more like 36 weeks instead of 37, so we only have about 2 ½ or 3 weeks to go. A couple of months ago, the thought of that would have really freaked me out, but now I'm starting to think, "Okay—let's do this!"

-November 13, 2007

It's a good thing that I adopted an attitude of "let's do this!" because it turned out that we did "do this" only days after that journal entry.

On Thursday, November 15, Stephen came home from work early to take me to the hospital for another non-stress test. I wasn't feeling great and was having some contractions—really nothing unusual at that point. After they'd hooked me up to the monitors I started having even more contractions. They were just a few minutes apart, and the nurses had me take an extra dose of Procardia. When that didn't slow things down, I received a shot of Brethine. And then another shot of Brethine. Stephen called to let someone know he probably wouldn't make it to his master's class that night, and after three-ish hours in the triage room, they decided to put me on an IV to make sure I was well-hydrated. Before they did, I asked to go to the bathroom, and as Stephen and I were getting me settled back into the bed, Nurse Tonya (one of my favorites!) told me not to get too comfortable—they were going to admit me.

We gathered my things and held my gown shut in the back with all of the cords hanging out as we walked (okay—I waddled) down the hall to room 1260. Nurse Dawn (another favorite and one of the head nurses—she ended up staying past her shift that night to make sure I was settled-in okay) started my IV and began the computer-paperwork for admitting me. I asked what the least amount of time was that I'd be in the hospital, thinking five or six more hours, and she said 24. Dr. K. ordered a magnesium sulfate drip for my IV, which was the strongest thing they could give me to relax my muscles and hopefully stop labor, and I received a shot of the steroid Celestone to accelerate the babies' lung development, should they arrive early. They would keep me on the magnesium sulfate for 24 hours so the girls would hopefully stay put long enough for me to receive a second steroid shot, and we would see where things were after that.

Turns out that magnesium sulfate is miserable stuff. I immediately felt weird once they started it in my IV, and before long I was feeling really hot. I felt so hot, in fact, that I would have bet the house that the heat was blowing in the room. I had no blankets on me and was just in my little hospital gown and was burning up. I kept drinking LOTS of ice water, which shouldn't have been necessary because I was staying hydrated through the IV. Stephen went out to get our dog settled with our neighbors and to get some food for us, since it was past dinner time once I was all checked-in. After calling our families and eating, we got ready for bed. Thankfully, we were in one of the nice birthing suites with a sleeper-loveseat; I gave Stephen all of my blankets, and he still slept with his clothes on and his hooded sweatshirt over his head! I did not sleep AT ALL. Okay, to be completely honest, I fell asleep for about 15 minutes around 4 a.m., only to be woken up by a wicked contraction, but otherwise I did not sleep at all. Besides having a lot on my mind—not wanting our babies to be born too early—the drugs kept me awake. I think Tiffany was my nurse that night, and she came in periodically to check on me, get more water for me, etc. Among other things, she had to check my reflexes because the mag can apparently affect that, too.

The next morning, I was feeling completely awful. I thought it was just the sleep deprivation, but I later realized that it was mostly the mag. My sinuses became clogged so I had to breathe through my mouth, causing me to constantly have a dry mouth—more water! Even my jaw muscles had become relaxed, making it difficult to chew anything tougher than a green bean. At some point, I realized my legs were swelling—my left leg became so swollen it was difficult to bend. I could barely walk without assistance, even though I was only going a few feet away to the bathroom. And my eyes were swollen—something I attributed to crying Friday morning after Dr. K. came in to visit, but that swelling, too, was mostly due to the mag. My contractions had only slowed but hadn't stopped, and he didn't think they would. He thought our girls might be born over the weekend. He wouldn't be on call, but said he might come in to do the C-section anyway—that he'd be around. (That made us feel good.) He told us about what we could expect if the girls had to be delivered—they would possibly need some oxygen, wouldn't have their suck-swallow reflex yet (and thus wouldn't be able to eat on their own), would probably need to be in incubators, and would likely need to stay in the hospital for 2-3 weeks. We probably wouldn't have more severe problems and need to go to the higher-level NICU in OKC, but we wouldn't know for sure until they were born. I'd made it 34 weeks, and that was a good thing.

It was really hard to think of our babies having to be hooked up to all kinds of equipment when they were born. You have this romanticized picture in your mind of your baby (or babies in our case) being born and holding them in your arms, gazing at them, taking in their first moments on earth, and to think that none of that will happen is really hard. Add to that what it means for them to have to be hooked up to machines—that they're not healthy—plus elevated hormones, magnesium sulfate, the pain/discomfort of hours of labor, and sleep deprivation, and you definitely have a case worthy of tears. Friday was a hard day.

A few of high points on Friday—Stephen came to sit on the edge of my bed one time and accidentally sat on a tube of KY jelly that one of the nurses had left on my bed and had become hidden under the sheets. It squirted all over him and the floor, making us both laugh. Dana and Melanie came to visit and brought lunch, magazines, snacks, and flowers. It cheered me up a lot to see them, even though I felt just about as rotten after they left. And, right next door, another friend was delivering her baby boy, so that was exciting. She still doesn't believe me when I tell her that I heard absolutely nothing! Maybe it was the mag, but I really think they just did a fantastic job insulating those walls.

At some point during the day, I asked Stephen to please just turn off the heat. He said, "Sweetie, the heat isn't on. That's the air that's blowing, and it's about 60 degrees in here." Yikes. When 24 hours had finally passed, they gave me another Celestone shot and took me off the mag. I was absolutely amazed at how quickly I felt better. It was like a fog had lifted. I could breathe normally again. I suddenly didn't feel so hot—and asked Stephen if the room had been that cold all along. (It had.) After a while I could chew normally again. My legs continued to be swollen and uncomfortable, but I felt so much better than I had for the past 24 hours. They wanted to keep me overnight again, to see how I'd do with contractions once I was off the mag, and then see how I was doing in the morning.

The mag had not stopped the contractions, and being off the mag didn't miraculously stop them, either. I continued having contractions, probably about every 10-20 minutes, and they became stronger and stronger. Every time they started getting regular in timing (maybe one every 5-10 minutes), the nurses would come in and give me another shot of Brethine or some more Procardia, which had to be done pretty much as often as they were able to drug me. There was not a point at which we thought, "Maybe I'll get to go home;" it didn't take long to figure out that the contractions were not going to stop, and we would be there until the girls were born. We were just praying that they would stay put until at least Monday, when Dr. K. would be back—and every extra day they were inside me was invaluable in making it more likely that they would be healthy when they were born. (We were much more satisfied with Dr K.'s bedside manner and medical prowess than the on call/weekend OB.)

I think it was Friday night that the nurses let me take a bath, but they were very strict about me sitting in the tub, not being in there more than 20 minutes, and having lots of help getting in and out. I had to keep my right arm dry because of the IV, so Stephen had to help me. That night, my nurse offered me some Ambien to help me sleep, which was a God-send. I didn't sleep well exactly, but I slept.

We had more sweet visitors on Saturday, but after visiting with friends, the contractions would really kick in again. Any amount of excitement or activity would set them off. At that point, we realized we had to really limit my time with visitors. It was either Saturday or Sunday evening when we were watching TV that we found a really entertaining stand-up comedy routine with Frank Caliendo. We were laughing so hard, and it felt so good! Except that every time I'd start to laugh, I'd have contractions, so we had to change the channel. What a bummer.

Saturday evening, I was really upset about the contractions coming back so strong. My dear friend, Katie, got married that night. She had asked me to be one of her bridesmaids, which I'd obviously had to decline, and my parents were at the wedding. They called us from the reception, and Katie, even as the busy bride, wanted to talk to me. I couldn't get on the phone with any of them. I hated to not talk to them, but I knew I wouldn't be able to get a word out without just falling apart and bursting into tears. So I just told Stephen to congratulate her for me, and tell her that I would talk to her soon. She said afterwards that she knew then that I must have been feeling pretty awful to not talk to her on her wedding night.

On Sunday, my parents told Stephen that they couldn't stand it any longer—they were coming out. The original plan had been for my parents to wait until the girls were home, when we'd really need their help, but they couldn't wait any longer. They knew that we needed them, and they needed to be with us to see that we were all *okay. Stephen did a pretty good job maintaining an even keel throughout this challenging time, but they knew him well enough to sense over the phone that we were about out of gas, keeping these babies inside as their little lungs developed. When he got off the phone and told me they were coming, we both broke down and cried. We were both so tired, so physically tired and emotionally exhausted. We had really needed to call in the cavalry, and they decided to come before we could ask. They and my sister, Allison, would arrive from Georgia on Wednesday.*

As time went on, the contractions went from feeling like a really uncomfortable tightening sensation to being a debilitating tightening sensation to being that and somewhat painful to being full-out tightening and crazy painful. I was having back labor, and I tried one time to shift positions and it only made it worse. I remember one time in particular, waking up with such a strong contraction and needing Stephen to coach me through it, but I didn't have the extra strength to do anything but whisper his name to try to wake him up. I think I finally coughed out a "Stephen!" loudly enough to wake him and get him by my side. At some point they started giving me pain meds to help me, but it's not like I was on an epidural or something. Yuck. And I had horrible heartburn—not something that had plagued me during my pregnancy until I was in the hospital. I asked for some Tums, and it seemed to take forever to get them! I guess they had to get Dr. K. to "prescribe" them for me; I wished I'd had Stephen walk across the parking lot to Walgreens and just buy me a bottle.

By Sunday night, we were completely exhausted. I had obviously had it by then—I'd been in labor since THURSDAY—and Stephen was tired of seeing his dear wife in such misery. As hard as it was to think of our girls coming early, by that point we knew it was only a matter of hours or days and were praying that Dr. K. would go ahead and deliver them on Monday. When he came in Monday morning, I think Stephen was ready to strong-arm him into doing whatever he had to do to get the babies out of me, but when he checked, I was dilated four centimeters. "It's time!" he said. That was at around 7:30 am, and he said he'd get an operating room booked and we'd do the c-section at about 9:00. We talked some, he sent in the head nursery nurse to prepare me for what would likely happen with the girls, and then one of my nurses came in to prepare me for surgery. Nothing to eat, nothing to drink, lots of papers to sign. Monday, November 19, 2007.

Delivery

Will I be able to deliver twins the old-fashioned way?

Maybe...

The answer to this will depend on so many things: your body, the position of your babies when you go into labor, how early and healthy your babies are, your doctor and his/her comfort level... Definitely talk to your obstetrician about this one.

I'm very petite, and my mom had c-sections with both my sister and me, so I figured that the odds of me delivering twins vaginally were pretty slim. My doctor was willing to try it, if the circumstances were right, but the circumstances did not end up being right for us.

Like all women's labor and delivery stories, each twin mama's story is different. Some women deliver naturally at 37 or 38 weeks with no complications whatsoever. Some women deliver one baby vaginally, then have to have a c-section because the second baby is breach. Some women labor for hours, and then have a c-section. I labored for 3 ½ days, and then had a c-section. (By the way, I asked the labor and delivery nurses, "So, when women talk about being in labor for 15 hours or 36 hours or whatever, does this count? Have I been in labor this whole time?" The answer was YES.) It wasn't until after it was all over that I asked my doctor, "Could I have delivered them naturally?" I think that if there had been no other way, I could have mustered the strength, but after being in labor for so long, I was too exhausted for my doctor to want me to try it.

Having a c-section was not the most fun thing ever, but it was not as bad as I thought. Mostly I was worried about "missing out" on the vaginal delivery experience/holding my babies right away, etc., but when it was over I was just thankful that we were all okay and overjoyed to see my babies when that moment came. It seems like people who struggle most with that issue are those who never anticipated having to have a c-section— mentally preparing yourself for that possibility can go a long way toward helping you have a positive experience no matter what.

Surprisingly, I had felt so uncomfortable and yucky beforehand that I actually felt *better* after having a c-section. I was definitely sore for a while, had trouble sitting myself up from lying down for a while, and I felt very nervous about taking off the dressing—the incision freaked me out and I had to get Stephen to help me with that—but the c-section wasn't debilitating (past a couple of days). My scar is barely noticeable, is below the bikini line, and is horizontal so it blends in with the natural creases that are there from bending over. (Awesome job, Dr. K.!) I don't remember for sure, but it seems that I was getting around reasonably well within a week and was basically (though not completely) back to normal by the time we took the girls home when they were two weeks old.

Before I knew it, they were wheeling me in my bed to the O.R. Stephen met me in there, once he was decked-out in his daddy-to-be scrubs, and Nurse Tonya was going to be Dr. K.'s right-hand gal. She held me as the anesthesiologist put in my spinal block, and then they had me back on the table, dressing me for surgery. Stephen was at my head, holding my hand, and everything was going well. But when Dr. K. began to cut, I could feel it. I asked, "Should I be feeling that?!" They waited a minute to make sure the drugs had had a chance to kick-in, then Dr. K. began cutting again. I could still feel it. "That's sharp!" They tried adding a local anesthetic, but when that didn't do it, Dr. K. quickly decided to put me under general anesthesia. So on the mask went, Stephen had to leave the O.R., and they knocked me out.

Some period of time later, I was in recovery, and a nurse was helping me wake up. I asked if the babies were okay, and she assured me they were. As I was groggily waking up, Stephen appeared, and told me that they were beautiful. Then he went back to the girls—and I was glad he did—as I was wheeled in my bed to my new room. (No more cushy labor-and-delivery suite in case someone in labor came in and needed it, but the regular women's center room was plenty nice.) Stephen came and went, checking on me and giving me updates about our baby girls. He called our families to tell them our news: The girls and I were healthy, Baby A had been born at 9:14 a.m., weighing 4 lbs. 11.6 oz., 17. 5 inches, and Baby B had been born at 9:15 a.m., weighing 4 lbs. 8.1 oz., 18.5 inches. We would wait to name them after I had had a chance to meet them.

Recovering from a c-section and having babies in the NICU

The time following the girls' birth is pretty fuzzy to me, as I was coming out of general anesthesia, but at some point Annette arrived and sat with me while Stephen went back-and-forth between the girls and me. Before she got there, I was getting pretty annoyed at times because Stephen would be gone so long and I was dying to hear about our babies! They wouldn't let me go anywhere for a while, and the girls couldn't come to me because of the care they were receiving in the NICU. (As a matter of fact, they did not leave the nursery at all until about ten days later, when they were allowed to come to my hospital room for the weekend before we took them home.) For a few minutes, Baby B was under an oxygen mask, and then for a few hours, Baby A was under an oxygen tent. The nurses told Stephen that originally they thought Baby B would have needed the tent and that Baby A's oxygen level was looking strongest, but after only 20 minutes or so they swapped (preview of the months and years to come!) Their heart rates, blood-oxygen levels, and body temperatures were being closely monitored (and would continue to be for many more days). The nurse had Stephen hold oxygen masks close to their noses and from time-to-time put the oxygen on their faces if the level started to decrease any, but the whole time their levels were really promising. Stephen thinks maybe they were just trying to keep him busy or trying to get him used to taking care of them. They were under heating lamps to make sure they stayed warm enough. But they were healthy and strong. I did not need to worry. But when could I see them?

FINALLY, at about 1:40 that afternoon, one of the nurses came to my room and said that Dr. K. had said I could go see them if I wanted to. Yes! Annette was there, and she helped the nurse get me from the bed to a wheelchair—IV, catheter bag, and all. They wheeled me to the nursery—the back part of the nursery where they have the babies who need extra- special equipment and attention— and there I met my girls. It makes me tear-up to think about it. Baby A was still under her tent, but Baby B was just lying on her special heat-lamp bed. I got to touch each of them, and they let me hold Baby B. Every time I see the pictures of those first moments with them, it makes me cry. What a memory.

After not long enough, I started to feel woozy, so they took me back to my room to rest. Honestly, I had felt so awful during the last days and weeks of my pregnancy, post-surgery felt pretty good. They had brought me a tray of clear liquid foods, but said I could eat real food as soon as I was ready—and I was. I ate and napped, Stephen came back and forth—and after seeing them finally, I was happy for him to spend more time by their sides than by mine—and I was able to periodically go see them, too.

That evening, on one of Stephen's visits to my room, we looked back over our list of names and decided to go with the ones we had picked out as our favorites. They fit. And it was easy to decide who was who. Baby A had spent several hours under the oxygen tent— she'd had to fight a little more—so we named her Caroline, "little and strong." Her middle name would be Dorothy, after Stephen's paternal grandmother. We named Baby B Abigail, "father's joy," and her middle name would be Marilyn after my paternal grandmother. We called our families to share that bit of news, and our fathers in particular were delighted with our choices. (Stephen had the pleasure of telling his grandmother over the phone on her 90th birthday that she had a great-granddaughter named after her. My grandmother had passed away many years before, but I could hear the tears in my daddy's eyes when we told him Abigail had been named after her.)

Interestingly, the Baby A and Baby B thing ended up opposite what they had termed them in utero. The doctors and ultrasound techs always called Baby A the one on the left, and Baby B the one on the right, but when they're born, they name them according to who comes out first. Abigail was already trying to work her way out (which explains why the shape of their heads looked quite different for a while after birth) and would have been born first if I'd delivered them naturally, so Caroline was easiest to pull out first via c-section and ended up being "Baby A." In all of our ultrasounds, though, it's the opposite. When people ask, "Who's oldest?" we tell them it's a tie.

Over the next several days, I felt better and better—minus some minor bumps in the road that night that the girls were born. For some reason, they decided not to give me drugs before the anesthesia wore off, so I was feeling pretty great, moving around on my own relatively well, and then BAM! That anesthesia wore off and I felt like my insides were ripping apart. I literally thought that my incision had ripped open. Once the Percocet finally kicked in, I was feeling much better, still extremely sore, but not with that horrific pain that I felt between the time that the anesthesia wore off and they gave me something else. Lesson learned: Always take the follow-up pain killer before the anesthesia has time to wear off!

That situation was aggravated, no doubt, by the fact that a few hours after they removed my catheter (and how great was it for a while not to have to go to the bathroom after 8+ months of constantly having to pee!), I felt the urge to pee, but then didn't actually go. Up and down from the bed, up and down from my wheel chair, up and down from the potty, and no tinkle. After a few hours of this, I really had to go. The nurses were checking up on me, asking me all of those prodding post-op questions, and when I still hadn't gone at almost midnight, Nurse Annette (not to be confused with my dear friend, Annette) re-catheterized me, and oh my goodness—I don't remember the exact quantity that came out, but it filled an entire pee-pee container and she had to grab another to get the rest. It was something like 1.2 liters, and she said that at around 400 mL you feel the urge, and at about 800 mL you feel desperate. No wonder I'd been so miserable! Turns out I'd gotten a tiny blood clot in there that was plugging up the works, which resolved itself when she re-cathed me. I was sure to go soon thereafter so another clot wouldn't have time to form! A side note: Nurse Annette who ran my catheter for me that night was in labor herself while taking care of me and had her baby the next morning! Wow.

The breast milk fortifier that was prescribed in the hospital was also available by special order in our pharmacy. Our pediatrician had us continue to add the fortifier to their bottles for several days after we brought our babies home from the hospital.

For the next few days, I recovered in my room and went to see the girls whenever I could. They were doing great. Still in the incubators to keep their body temps regulated, still eating from feeding tubes, and still being constantly monitored, but doing great. The hospital lactation consultant hooked me up with the hospital's breast pump, and I started pumping every three hours so the girls could get some mommy milk through their feeding tubes. Their suck-swallow reflexes had not developed yet, though we tried every day to see if they would nurse or at least take a bottle. They added some breast milk fortifier to *what I gave them so they'd get extra protein and hopefully gain weight a little faster.*

On Wednesday, my family arrived, and we were overjoyed to see them, as they were to see us and their new family members. And on Thursday, Thanksgiving Day, I was released from the hospital. They kept my room for me, though, so we would have a place to stay when we were visiting the girls. We had Thanksgiving Dinner in my hospital room—thanks to the nurses giving us the extra meal trays that people didn't use because they checked out early to be home on Thanksgiving. We wanted to take a picture of the five of us crammed into my hospital room with those big cafeteria trays full of food, eating Thanksgiving dinner, but none of us could move to get the camera! We all went back to our house that afternoon, and I took a nap. When I woke up, I was absolutely itching to get back to the hospital, to my babies. My dad was making dinner for us, and after somewhat patiently waiting about 30 minutes, I asked, "Are we eating now or later?" "Why?" he asked, "What time did you want to go back?" "About 30 minutes ago," I said. They were all so sorry I'd been freaking out about going back, and pushed Stephen and me out the door to be on our way and said we could eat later. That was a Thanksgiving I'll never forget. We had SO much to be thankful for.

The NICU thing was emotionally trying, but it was okay. And in the grand scheme of things, a couple of weeks is not that long (although I know it seems like it right now). The head nursery nurse scared me half to death with "worst case scenario" talk a couple of days before the girls were born, and I was hysterical at the thought of our girls having to be hooked up to machines. But even having to see them with feeding tubes and in incubators wasn't terrible—we were more overcome with joy and adoration for them than we were upset by the monitors they had to be hooked up to. Should you find yourself with babies in the NICU, http://www.nicuawareness.org/ is a great place to find resources and support on how to be involved in their care, feeding your babies in the NICU, and what to expect and how to manage life when you take your preemies home.

It was wonderful to get a chance to nearly fully recover before they came home, but it killed me to be away from them. One night, we had gone back to the hospital for the last time that day, and Caroline was crying. I held her out of her incubator for a while, and she calmed down, but I had to put her back because she needed to be in there to stay warm. She began crying again as soon as I put her back, and then I cried the whole way out of the hospital and the whole way home. (I had some real issues stemming from that for several weeks after they came home—it was really difficult for me to hear them cry and not run to them, even more so, I think, than it is for most mommies.) They had to stay a full two weeks, so we went back-and-forth for about eight days—from the time I was released until the following Friday, when the head nursery nurse said we could have the girls in our room and spend the weekend with them in the hospital with the nursing staff there if we needed them, before taking them home hopefully on Sunday or Monday.

That weekend, we were finally able to be together as our new little family. My parents had had to leave the Thursday before. It was really hard to say goodbye, I think mostly because of my raging hormones and the fact that I'd developed a mysterious fever (probably mastitis that had not yet shown other symptoms) and felt awful, but also because it made me so sad to think of them having to say goodbye to their grandbabies! I don't dissolve into tears every time we part ways anymore, but it is much more difficult living far apart now than it was before the girls were born.

Anyway, that weekend in the hospital with the girls in our room was wonderful in ways and stressful in ways. We knew they couldn't leave until we could feed them on our own, and they had JUST figured out how to drink from bottles. (It took almost a month for them to learn to nurse—when they were at 38 weeks gestational age.) Feeding them went well until it was time to burp, and then we had the hardest time getting them to burp! And they couldn't eat more until they'd gotten rid of the gas in their tummies. I was almost in tears (thank you, postpartum hormones) every time we couldn't get one of them to burp, for fear that we wouldn't be able to take them home Sunday or Monday as we'd hoped. Finally, though, they'd burp—a couple of times we'd ask a nurse to come in and help us, and they showed us some tricks to get them to burp. It was definitely a silver lining to the extended hospital stay to learn from the nurses for two weeks. They are literally pros! In that respect, it made us almost feel sorry for people who "have" to take their babies home within 24 hours of their birth—at least we felt relatively competent as care-takers by the time we were allowed to take the girls home.

On Sunday, December 2, after eating regularly and consistently gaining weight for a few days, Caroline and Abigail came home! On the way home, Stephen asked, "So what are we going to do when we get home with them?" I replied that I didn't really know exactly how it would go, but I figured they'd keep us busy. Life hasn't slowed down since.

•6•

"You're breastfeeding twins?!"

First of all, I am a big proponent of breastfeeding, but please read the following remembering that my greatest desire is that you be a *sane* mama—not one who is stressed out over the logistics of breastfeeding twins. I hope that this chapter will provide some tips and encouragement to make breastfeeding more do-able for you, but rest assured that how "good" a mother you are is not dependent upon where your babies' milk comes from.

Breastfeeding was something I always knew I wanted to do because I knew it was supposed to be the healthiest thing for my baby (or bab*ies* as it turned out) and would be healthy for me, and it seemed to me that if this was what God had in mind for baby nutrition, I wouldn't be able to beat it with human-designed formula. I had the attitude that I *wanted* to breastfeed; the more I learned about the benefits, the more determined I became that I *would* breastfeed.

Why should I consider breastfeeding?

Even after learning that we were expecting twins, I still wanted to nurse our girls, and meeting other moms who had done it solidified my belief that I could, too. After all, women had done this with twins for hundreds and even thousands of years, right? Sure, we all know people who have exclusively formula-fed their babies and they turned out just fine, and while formula seems to provide adequate nutrition for babies, there are about a gazillion things in breast milk that cannot be duplicated in formula. As my pregnancy progressed, I learned more and more about the benefits of breastfeeding that really blew my mind and still amaze me. A few that I remember are:

- Breastfeeding builds a stronger immune system for baby (especially important for preemies).[7] You're passing on immunities to your baby against germs that you fight off while nursing and against illnesses you actually get while nursing— it's very unlikely that you'll give your baby your cold/flu/etc. while you're nursing.
- Breastfeeding reduces the risk of diabetes[8], obesity[9], and a host of other things for baby that he or she will benefit from for the rest of his or her life.
- Breastfeeding reduces the risk of breast and ovarian cancer for mom[10].
- Breastfeeding provides amazing post-pregnancy weight loss for mom—it burns around 500 calories *per baby* per day[11].

[7] Hanson, L. Å, Korotkova, M., Lundin, S., Håversen, L., Silfverdal, S., Mattsby-Baltzer, I., . . . Telemo, E. (2003). The Transfer of Immunity from Mother to Child. Annals of the New York Academy of Sciences, 987(1), 199-206. doi:10.1111/j.1749-6632.2003.tb06049.x

[8] Martens, P. J., Shafer, L. A., Dean, H. J., Sellers, E. A., Yamamoto, J., Ludwig, S., . . . Shen, G. X. (2016). Breastfeeding Initiation Associated With Reduced Incidence of Diabetes in Mothers and Offspring. *Obstetrics & Gynecology,* 1. doi:10.1097/aog.0000000000001689

[9] WHO | Exclusive breastfeeding to reduce the risk of childhood overweight and obesity. (2014, September). Retrieved October 21, 2016, from http://www.who.int/elena/titles/bbc/breastfeeding_childhood_obesity/en/

[10] Breastfeeding lowers your breast cancer risk | MD Anderson ... (2014, October). Retrieved October 21, 2016, from https://www.mdanderson.org/publications/focused-on-health/october-2014/breastfeeding-breast-cancer-prevention.html

[11] Benefits Of Breastfeeding For Baby & Mother | Cleveland Clinic. (2016, March

- Breastfeeding releases progesterone, which contracts your uterus, getting things back in shape faster.[12] It also keeps menstruation/pregnancy at bay while nursing. (But do not rely on it as your only form of birth control!)

The more I learn about breastfeeding, the more amazed I am, and the more it stands as yet another example to me of God's incredible design and plan. To find many more benefits, check out the website for La Leche League at http://www.llli.org/ These folks are so gung-ho about breastfeeding that they have an organization for it. (Beware—some of these women also advocate breastfeeding for YEARS, something that is a little extreme for most people. Their website is an excellent source of information, though.)

Will I be able to produce enough milk for two babies?

Yes. Yet another awesome thing about breastfeeding is the way a mother can produce as much milk as her baby—or babies in this case—demand. Can some things get in the way of this miracle? Yes. Stress can definitely reduce your ability to produce enough milk—kind-of ironic, when you think about how stressful it can be to have a new baby or two in the first place, isn't it? The only time my girls cried from hunger after I had just nursed was at a bedtime feeding at the end of a very stressful two weeks. My husband comforted me while *I* cried, we gave the girls bottles, they went to sleep, and then we did what we could to reduce my stress level. Review the section on Helping Hands in Chapter 2 for reminders on how having good helpers can reduce your stress. Also, read ahead in Chapter 7 about schedules: Not only will getting your babies into an eating and sleeping routine be good for your general sanity, but feeding them on a consistent schedule will help train your body to know how much milk to make, when it's needed, and you won't have to worry about

10). Retrieved October 21, 2016, from http://my.clevelandclinic.org/health/diseases_conditions/hic_am_i_pregnant/hic-the-benefits-of-breastfeeding-for-baby-and-for-mom

[12] Benefits Of Breastfeeding For Baby & Mother | Cleveland Clinic. (2016, March 10). Retrieved October 21, 2016, from http://my.clevelandclinic.org/health/diseases_conditions/hic_am_i_pregnant/hic-the-benefits-of-breastfeeding-for-baby-and-for-mom

not having enough to go around.

Try not to stress about how much your babies are eating at each feeding. Babies do not over-eat; when they have had enough, they refuse to eat any more, so don't worry that they're eating *too much*. Unless your pediatrician tells you to monitor how many ounces they're taking in at each feeding because she's concerned that they aren't gaining enough weight, you also do not need to worry that they aren't eating *enough*—they'll keep eating at a feeding until they aren't hungry anymore. When they stop eating, that means they have had an adequate amount for that feeding. Again, the irony is that the more you stress about these things, the less milk you'll actually be able to provide, so trust that mommy-nature is taking care of this unless your pediatrician tells you otherwise.

Is all of this to say that you will never, ever have to supplement with formula? No. Most of us do at some time or another for some reason or another. In all likelihood, though, you can generally produce enough milk to breastfeed twins.

How will I get started?

You'll also find good info at the La Leche League site on *how* to breastfeed. Another good resource is this website from the Stanford University School of Medicine. Our pediatrician at the time that our girls were newborns had completed his residency at Stanford and recommended this site: http://newborns.stanford.edu/Breastfeeding/ABCs.html

Thankfully, there will be someone at the hospital who is a certified lactation consultant or at the very least a nurse (or several nurses) who can give you expert coaching on how to get your babies to latch on, how to operate a breast pump, and other things that new moms generally have no idea how to do. It is such a blessing that hospitals keep these people on staff because it's impossible to really know what to do from reading a book. Expect these folks to handle your boobs in a way that was previously reserved for your most intimate relationships. You

> As natural as breastfeeding is, it's something that you've never done before, and it really doesn't come as easily or naturally for many of us as we expect it to. But hang in there! It is totally worth it.

probably won't feel violated, though, and will be thankful for the help—as natural as breastfeeding is, it's something that you've never done before, and it really doesn't come as easily or naturally for many people as they expect it to. It may take several days for your babies to latch on properly and really get a full meal when nursing, and it'll probably be a few weeks before you start to feel really comfortable with the whole operation, but hang it there! It is totally worth it.

Lactation consultants will also commonly do home-visits, hold breastfeeding support groups, and provide telephone support after you leave the hospital. Your hospital staff members are an excellent resource for finding a local lactation consultant, but if you need to search elsewhere, try the International Lactation Consultant Association's website www.ilca.org or Breastfeeding.com, which boasts the "largest directory of lactation consultants anywhere." I cannot encourage you enough to seek the advice of a lactation consultant when you hit a bump in the road—I say *when* and not *if,* because most breastfeeding moms struggle with it at one time or another. If you experience difficulty, it could be due to any of a myriad of issues: your babies not latching on properly, you have an overactive letdown reflex, engorgement... Lactation consultants know boob-issues like no one else, and I hope you'll consult with one of them—immediately—when the going gets rough.

It makes me so sad to hear people say that they tried for three days, but their babies wouldn't nurse, so they had to give them formula. For one thing, in the first few days newborns don't eat that much anyway—all they need is the little bit of that first milk that mommy produces (colostrum) and they're fine anyway. Secondly, many—if not most—women need some help learning how to breastfeed. I can't help but wonder if these moms might have had greater success if they'd had better support and better resources—it does make a difference!

When we brought our girls home from the hospital, they still couldn't nurse—and I had tried at least once a day, every day, for two weeks at that point already. My girls were born at 34 weeks and did not yet have their suck-swallow reflex, which normally kicks in sometime around the 36-week mark. They were

> You can still breastfeed if your babies are born before their suck-swallow reflex kicks in!

on feeding tubes for about 10 days (during which time I pumped every three hours around the clock so they'd have mommy milk in their feeding tubes and so my body would be accustomed to producing enough milk to nurse them when they were ready), and then they could only drink from bottles for a while. When I tried to nurse, they would sort-of mouth around, but never even came close to latching-on.

I continued to try every day at home—sometimes with tears welling-up in my eyes as my babies would not take my breast. I can't remember if I called our hospital lactation consultant for advice, or if she had told me this before we left the hospital and it took me a while to remember it, but what finally worked was using a plastic nipple shield. (Ask for a nipple shield at the hospital if you have to leave before your babies are able to nurse. Medela manufactures one, which can be purchased on Amazon.com, among other places.) It mimicked the feel of the bottle nipple, and after several days or maybe even a week or two of them successfully using the nipple shield, I tried having them nurse without it and they did great nursing naturally from that point on. They were a month old (38 weeks gestational age) by the time they were really able to breastfeed.

It takes more energy, though, for a baby to nurse than to drink from a bottle, so we had to transition them from full-time bottle-feeding to full-time breastfeeding. Our pediatrician was concerned that if they nursed full-time they would burn too many calories and not gain weight the way they needed to, and so he advised me to alternate between breast and bottle for several more weeks. They were three months old (equivalent to six-week-old full-term babies) before they were nursing 100% of the time. Yes, I was determined!

I'm not sure that I would have kept trying to breastfeed if it hadn't been for my very supportive husband and a few other champions in my corner. My husband and I had discussed ahead of time all of the benefits of breastfeeding and my deep desire to provide those benefits to our babies, and so he knew that I might regret it if I threw in the towel. It was hard for him to see me struggle, and he might have told me to go ahead and give them formula if he hadn't known how badly I had wanted breastfeeding to work and all of the benefits there would be for all of us if we could make it work. He couldn't do anything to physically help me, but he could remind me that our babies were still not even newborn-age yet and encourage me not to give up—and I didn't. If it is your intention to breastfeed your babies, make sure you have someone (or several someones) in your corner to champion your efforts. There will be times that it isn't easy, but if you are determined, you can almost certainly do it. Having your husband, your mother, and/or a close friend or two to encourage you to keep trying may make the difference. And even if you find that your babies really won't nurse, which does occasionally happen, the benefits of breast milk are so great that I hope that you will consider pumping and feeding breast milk to your babies in bottles. Is it a lot of work? Yes. Will it be worth it? Yes.

Besides being your champion, your husband can be a tremendous help in your nursing efforts by taking care of *you* — ask him in advance to help you remember to eat enough and drink enough, and ask him take care of things around the house that might cause you stress. You will be more successful if he shares this goal with you!

All of that said, having a sane mama trumps all of that other stuff. **If you find that breastfeeding and/or pumping is going to push you over the edge, choose your sanity instead.** Talk to your pediatrician about the best formula for your babies, and rest assured that formula plus sane mama beats breast milk plus stressed out/crazy mama any day.

How Will I Breastfeed TWO Babies at Once?

As far as the logistics of nursing twins are concerned, the main question is: How? Do I nurse them simultaneously, or one at a time? This is totally up to you and what you're able to manage. I have known women who could nurse their babies at the same time, and my hat's off to them. I managed to do it a few times, but I personally found it very cumbersome—maybe this is because I'm so petite— and it made me feel even more like a dairy cow than I already did. Plus, even though they didn't have reflux per se, if I didn't burp them promptly/*immediately*, they would spit up quite a bit, and I couldn't figure out how to sit one up quickly to burp while the other was still latched on—perhaps if I'd been an octopus or at least had an extra person around all the time that would have helped. And I really enjoyed the intimacy of nursing each of them individually. That was special to me, and because I was not working and did not have older kids to tend to, I had the luxury of the time it takes to nurse one at a time. And it does take a LOT of time. You will most definitely want to use a Boppy or other nursing pillow, although a regular throw pillow or bed pillow works well, too. If you want to try nursing simultaneously, you may shop online for a nursing pillow specially designed for twins—MyBrestFriend is a good one. If you are interested in nursing them simultaneously, I encourage you to try it and to try as many positions as you can come up with—a quick online search for "twins breastfeeding hold" will yield 16 million results—no exaggeration. Be prepared that it may be a while before you and the babies are comfortable enough with nursing for you to try to tackle nursing them at the same time.

You will read or hear somewhere and quickly notice when you start nursing that you will likely produce more milk on one side than the other. This is easy enough for singleton moms to compensate for by alternating which side they nurse on first at each feeding—at the first feeding of the day, feed the baby on the left side for 10-15 minutes, and then switch to the right side for the last 10-15 minutes; at the next feeding, nurse on the right side first and then the left. I read somewhere that a mom kept a safety pin on one side of her bra or the other to remind her which side to start on at the next feeding.

When nursing twins, you don't want to switch breasts mid-feeding. If you do, the first baby will get all of the first milk from both breasts, and then leave his brother with leftovers. (The quality/substance of breast milk changes through each feeding[13], and each baby needs to get *both* the foremilk *and* the hindmilk at each feeding.) With twins, you will need to do a complete feeding on one boob for each baby. But you still need to alternate which baby nurses on which side at each feeding, because you're trying to keep things equitable between two babies—if your left side always produces more, you don't want one baby to get his first or hungriest feeding of the day on the left side every day, leaving the other baby to always get his hungriest feeding on the lesser-producing side. Also, one

---

[13] Mohrbacher, M., IBCLC, FILCA. (n.d.). Difference Between Foremilk And Hindmilk? - TheBump.com. Retrieved October 21, 2016, from http://www.thebump.com/a/difference-between-foremilk-and-hindmilk

baby may be a heartier sucker than the other, and you don't want your boobs to end up producing even more differently because you're consistently stimulating one side more than the other.

I always nursed on the left side at the first feeding of the day. On one day, I'd wake and feed Baby A first (left side for her first feeding that day), and then wake and feed Baby B (right side for her first feeding that day), and then alternate through the day so that Baby A's second feeding would be on the right, and Baby B's would be on the left, and so on. The next day, Baby B would go first all day, nursing first on the left at her first feeding, then on the right at her next feeding, and so on. Having all of this to keep track of is another reason to keep a chart (see Appendix) of their feeding habits or use an app such as Baby Tracker Nursing App or Baby Connect so you don't get this all mixed up when you're trying to function on very little sleep. At least I didn't have to use a safety pin on my bra if I knew that I always started the day doing the first feeding on the left side.

Until your babies start eating solid food (at around 4-6 months, depending on your pediatrician's advice), they will need to nurse for about 20-30 minutes apiece. And at first, they will eat every three hours around the clock—yes, your math is correct, you are talking about nursing for more hours a day than you will sleep. Because our girls were preemies (as twins commonly are), our pediatrician strongly advised that I continue feeding them every three hours (to simulate the near-constant nutrition they would have received if they were still in the womb and to ensure healthy weight gain) for weeks longer than full-term babies have to do so. When we went to that six-week check-up and he said I could let them sleep for 4-5 hours at a time at night, it was like Christmas. At their eight-week check-up, we got the green light to let them sleep 6-8 hours—Hallelujah. But during the day, they continued to eat every three hours until they were about four and a half months old (adjusted age of three months old). After that, they could eat every four hours during the day.

I know all of this sounds like an eternity of nursing babies all the time, but it goes by really quickly. I was about ready to throw in the towel, though, at around six months. I was tired of spending so much time nursing, and we had started them on "solids" (very liquidy rice cereal and strained baby food is not very "solid" by most standards), which was adding another huge chunk of time to the already busy feeding schedule. Between nursing and spoon-feeding, I was spending six hours a day feeding them in some way, shape, or form, and I was sick of it. But just as I was about to wean them, they got much better and more efficient at it all—as they gained expertise at eating solid foods, they needed less breast milk, so instead of spending 20-30 minutes nursing every time, it went down to only about 10 minutes per baby per feeding. And then when I thought about preparing bottles and cleaning bottles (not to mention the exorbitant cost of formula), I decided to stick with it and ended up nursing our girls till they were a year old and could safely have cow's milk. They went straight from the breast to a cup without having a bottle (past the three-month mark when I stopped alternating breastfeeding and bottle-feeding).

> At around six months, the time your babies spend nursing each day will decrease, making it easier to continue nursing.

I recently stumbled upon a great resource for breastfeeding mothers. This Timeline of a Breastfed Baby has all kinds of details about what to expect in the first days of nursing, as well as what you and your nursing babies will be experiencing at monthly milestones through the first year. http://www.thealphaparent.com/2011/12/timeline-of-breastfed-baby.html

"Nipple confusion?"

By the way, I think the whole "nipple confusion" thing is a myth—as long as babies are used to both the breast and the bottle (and a pacifier for that matter) they seem to take just fine to both. Our girls alternated fine for months. It's once you give up one or the other that they may not go back to it. We tried to give them bottles of breast milk once after about six weeks away from bottles, and they didn't want any part of it. I'm sure if that had been their only option they would have learned, but that wasn't my intent so I didn't try again after that. We also had no "nipple confusion" with pacifiers. They know where their food is coming from!

Storing Breast Milk

A note about freezing breast milk: Breast milk storage bag packaging will give you some good guidelines for how long breast milk should keep in the refrigerator or freezer. We had some in the freezer, though, that *should* have still been good but had actually gone bad—which I didn't discover until after the girls had refused to drink it and I had a sip. I gagged, and felt horrible for having given our babies sour milk. Moral of the story: Taste thawed breast milk yourself before you feed it to your babies.

Burp those babies!

Whether your babies breastfeed or bottle-feed, they will not eat well unless they burp well. Think about it: We grown-ups burp without any effort because we eat sitting up, and the gas bubbles just work their way up and out—sometimes as gross man-belches, and sometimes as quiet little burps that we barely notice. Babies eat pretty-much lying down, so those bubbles need help getting out.

A few things are likely to happen if your babies don't burp during and after feedings: 1) They will not be able to eat as much as they'd like, because the gas bubbles get in the way of them eating more, which makes for cranky babies; 2) They will spit up a lot, because the gas bubbles get in the way of their food making it where it needs to go, and that makes for hungry, cranky babies; and 3) Those gas bubbles can become painful, which makes for cranky babies. Me, I like happy babies.

At the end of our girls' 12-day stay in the NICU, the nurses had us keep the babies in our hospital room for 48 hours before they would let us take them home, to make sure we could get them to eat and continue to gain weight. As you can imagine, the pressure was on—we desperately wanted to take our girls home, and so we desperately wanted them to eat! However, even though they would start eating pretty well from bottles, we had a hard time getting them to burp, and so we couldn't get them to take in enough food. With post-partum hormones in full bloom, this situation quickly stressed me out and had me in tears. The solution: The nurses came in, propped our babies up on their knees, supporting their little heads in their left hands (so they were in a sitting-up position), and firmly patted them on the back with their right hands until we heard an audible, obvious baby belch. We novice parents had been gently, barely petting their backs, with their heads on our shoulders—you know, like you see in movies or on TV—and then asking each other after every cute baby sound and grunt, "Was that a burp?" The nurses quickly taught us that if it doesn't sound like a burp, it isn't one, and that it takes a stronger pat than what we had been doing to get the burps out. Once our girls burped, they ate more, and we were able to take them home at the end of our 48-hour "trial period."

Ways to get babies to burp:

- The position described above is my favorite: Sit baby sideways on your lap, facing to the left, the side of Baby's head leaning against your chest (until he can hold up his own head), with his chin cradled in your left hand. Pat firmly on the back with your right hand. Sometimes a slight bounce of your knees helps, too. Lean baby forward a little, or lean him back a little, and pat some more, trying to adjust the angle of his tummy to get the burp out.
- Put baby on your left shoulder, a little higher up than you might think, so that your shoulder is putting some very gentle pressure on baby's tummy. (Not with baby hanging over your shoulder, though—that's too far.) Hold baby with your left hand and firmly pat with your right.
- Sometimes lifting baby with both hands under his arms (with your fingers supporting his head) so that his body can straighten out for a second helps work the bubbles into a more burp-able position.

Be sure to try to burp your babies at about the half-way point in each feeding, as well as at the end of each feeding. If they seem to want to stop eating, there is a good chance they need to burp, so try to burp them, and then see if they'd like to eat some more after that.

A little spit-up is okay!

As noted above, babies often spit up simply because they have some gas bubbles that need to come out—and when they do, sometimes food comes out with the air. Sometimes, babies eat to the point of "overflowing," and so they spit up some to get rid of the excess. Our babies spit up quite a bit—at least a little at almost every feeding, especially if I didn't burp them promptly—but they were still gaining weight the way they needed to, and so our pediatrician assured us that they were fine. If spit-up just kind-of spills out and baby doesn't seem to be bothered by it, then it is probably nothing to worry about. If it seems more like projectile vomiting, you may have cause for concern, or if your babies seem to spit up as much as they take in, many times a day, you should consult your pediatrician.

Feeding a Nursing Mom

Your pediatrician and obstetrician can consult with you about nutrition while breastfeeding, and there are books on the market solely devoted to this topic, not to mention thousands of articles on the web. (See http://www.breastfeedingplace.com/top-12-best-foods-to-eat-while-breastfeeding/) Generally speaking, the nutritional needs of nursing moms are very similar to those of pregnant moms: You still need to eat enough to sustain the dietary needs of you *and* your babies. Nursing moms should take in 400-500 extra calories per baby per day. Eat a lot, eat a wide variety of foods, include whole grains, protein, calcium, and drink plenty of fluids.[14]

Below is a recipe for egg custard, something my great-grandmother prepared for my grandmother after each of her babies was born, that my grandmother cooked for my mother after my sister and I were born, and that my mom made for me after our girls were born. (My great-grandmother had ten babies, all of whom were born before formula was invented and many of whom lived into their nineties!) Even if egg custard doesn't actually help mothers produce more and better milk, it's yummy and chock full of protein—you might as well ask someone to make it for you and enjoy!

Grandma's Egg Custard Pie
- 1 (9-inch) unbaked pie crust
- 3 eggs, beaten
- ¾ c. white sugar
- ¼ tsp. salt (ingredients continued on next page)

---

[14] Nutrition During Breastfeeding : Diet Considerations. (n.d.). Retrieved October 24, 2016, from http://americanpregnancy.org/breastfeeding/diet-considerations-while-breastfeeding/

- 1 tsp. vanilla extract
- 1 egg white
- 1 can evaporated milk + enough milk to add up to 2 ½ c.
- ¼ tsp. ground nutmeg

Preheat oven to 400°.

Mix together eggs, sugar, salt, and vanilla extract. Stir well. Blend in the evaporated milk and milk.

Line a pie pan with the pie crust, and brush inside the bottom and sides of the crust with egg white to prevent a soggy crust. Pour custard mixture into the crust, and sprinkle with nutmeg.

Bake 30-35 minutes, or until a knife inserted in the center comes out clean. Cool on a rack before cutting.

Breast Milk as Home Remedies

Here are some more awesome things I learned about breast milk after our girls were weaned—would have loved to try some of these while I was still nursing! Check with your doctor first, and then consider giving these home remedies a try:

Congestion Squirt two drops of your breast milk into each nostril, and then use an aspirator to clear baby's sinuses.

Minor abrasions Dab it on scrapes as an antibacterial agent.

Conjunctivitis For mild cases of pinkeye, two drops in each infected eye twice a day can be an effective antibiotic.

Eczema Use a cotton pad to blot dry spots with breast milk as a moisturizer.

What if I seriously cannot breastfeed?

As I said (and as you've ascertained by now), I am a big proponent of breastfeeding. I truly do think that the benefits are worth the effort. I do realize, though, that having a sane mama is more important for your babies than having breast milk, so if you find yourself having to choose between the two, go with the sane mama. They will be completely fine if all they ever have is formula, either because you are the rare case that physically cannot nurse them or because you feel that the effort may push you over the edge.

Moreover, if you decide to supplement breastfeeding with formula at night so someone else can take over nighttime feedings and buy you a little rest, or you are stressing that they might not be getting enough to eat and you can buy yourself some peace of mind by adding a little formula to their diets until they get better at nursing, they will be fine! I hope that you will give breastfeeding a go, but if you don't, you'll still deserve a medal for being a twin mama—period.

• 7 •

"I Don't Know How You Do It!"

The Daily Routine

"I don't know how you do it!" That will be one of the top comments you'll hear from people for a while. And trying to figure out *how we would do it* was one of the many things that overwhelmed me when we found out we were expecting twins. You know, many little girls grow up fantasizing about being a twin, and then a lot of us grow up to think it would be fun to have twins, but when I saw moms with twins, I generally thought, "Wow…that must be a lot of work." I have a sister who is ten years younger than I am, and I babysat a lot as a teenager, so I felt that becoming a mom at 28 and having to figure out how to care for our *one* baby was very doable. The thought of having *two* babies at the same time whose needs needed to be met around the clock totally freaked me out. Especially when every parenting book I picked up included only a few less-than-helpful pages on twins and multiples, highly recommending that we have family stay with us for several weeks and/or hire a night nanny. Not possible. Freak out.

As I said earlier in this book, if you can get {good!} help, then by all means, do. However, if your circumstances are like ours were, and having Grandma move in or paying for help is not an option, this chapter is the "here's what you're gonna do" chapter.

The key: Have a plan for getting those babies to sleep. Our friends and family gave us many great gifts when our girls were on the way, but the single greatest gift anyone gave us was the information we needed to get our babies to GO TO SLEEP. Having them hungry on a predictable time table will follow having them sleeping in a healthy pattern, which means far fewer episodes of two simultaneously crying, hungry and/or sleepy babies, and much greater sanity for Mom and Dad.

There are about as many parenting philosophies out there as there are parents and children. Regarding sleeping and eating, on one extreme you find parents who believe that their infant children should decide when they need to sleep, how long they need to sleep, where they need to sleep, when they should eat, how often they should eat, and so forth. I wish that I could tell you that I know people for whom that style has worked well, but the truth is that every single person I know who has prescribed to that type philosophy has had a really rough time getting their babies to sleep through the night on a consistent basis. Every. Single. One.

On the other extreme, you find people who believe in Nazi-like schedules by dictator parents who allow zero wiggle room for any reason. I don't actually know anyone whom I'd describe in those terms, but I have to admit that it does make sense to me that the parents should be in charge, not the babies. When friends of ours who had thriving, happy, healthy, well-rested children—and they, themselves, were thriving, happy, healthy, well-rested parents—told us that their children had always followed some type of sleep schedule, I listened. Why would I follow the advice of people who seem to be struggling? I think I'll listen to friends who seem to be getting this parenting thing "right."

Disclaimer: I have had some awesome parent-friends who have not stuck with much of a routine with their babies' sleeping and eating patterns, and I still love and respect them. They are brilliant, loving, fantastic people and wonderful parents, and they've had very good reasons for making the parenting decisions they've made (health issues, older children's school schedules, etc.) I have not known any of them to be fully satisfied with their children's sleep

habits, though. They often complain that their
don't sleep through the night, that their four-y
wake them up at 5:30 in the morning, and so for
they'd recommend that anyone intentionally duplic

I have also known plenty of parents who let thei
late into the evening. Again, some of them have v͟e͟ ͟ ͟g͟o͟o͟d͟ reasons
for this, and I respect their logic; however, they tend to complain
about how they have limited adult conversations with their spouses,
are exhausted and out of patience, etc. They also seem puzzled that,
even with late bedtimes, their children still wake up early in the
morning. As you'll probably discover for yourselves at some point,
keeping young children up late in the hope that they'll sleep later in
the morning almost never works—they'll probably still wake up
early, but without having had adequate rest.

My husband and I rarely went out on "dates" when our girls were
little, but almost every evening was a "date night in" because our
girls were in bed around 7:00 until they started kindergarten...and
then bedtime was at 7:30. An early bedtime makes it easier when
you do hire a babysitter—most of the times that we had a sitter when
the girls were babies, we'd have her come over as we were getting
the girls ready for bed (so they'd see her face and she'd be familiar
just in case they woke up), and then we'd leave after we'd already
put them to bed, making it easier on us, the girls, and our babysitter.
An early bedtime also enables you to have friends over to your home
and enjoy some adult company and conversation after your little
ones are in bed.

I could go on and on—suffice it to say that I *highly* encourage
you to try having your babies on some type of schedule, at least for
several weeks or a few months, to see if it works for you. There is no
one-size-fits-all approach to anything parenting, but I can't
encourage you enough to try what I'm about to lay out here. It's
worked well for countless others, and I hope it will work well for
you, too.

Where do I start?

First, decide that you are going to be in charge. Yes, you will be
unsuccessful at times, but generally you, not your babies, are going
to make the plans for your household. "Hello! Welcome to the
planet. I am your mommy, and this is your daddy, and we are here to

you how things are done." Do we know everything? Obviously . But we do have the advantage of having been on this planet for 0 years give-or-take, which makes us more qualified to make decisions than our babies who have been outside the womb for 30 days. That's the first premise.

Secondly, think about what you already know. As adults, we know that our body clocks get set by routine—by teaching our bodies to expect to wake and sleep at certain times, to eat at certain times, we get into a feel-good groove. If we want our children to fall into healthy sleeping and eating patterns sooner rather than later—patterns that are also conducive to living in our families—then these routines need to be taught to them.

Our friends recommended books, which were very helpful in getting us on board with the idea that our babies—and we—would not only survive, but thrive, if we adopted some sort of routine. The book that we used as our starting-point for creating a schedule that would work for our family was *Baby Wise* by Gary Ezzo and Robert Bucknam[15]. I know that there on mixed reviews on this book; people seem to either absolutely hate it or absolutely love it, depending on whether they believe strongly in demand-feeding their infants or feeding them on more of a schedule. The thing is that if you have twins, do not have live-in help, and want to maintain your sanity, feeding them on demand is not really an option. *Baby Wise* was highly recommended to me by friends who had singletons as well as friends who had multiples—parents who had well-rested, pleasant, happy children—and I highly recommend it to all new parents. As with all books (including mine!) common sense must be applied, as well as the ability to take from it what will work for your family; I don't believe that any single self-help book or anyone else's opinion can be the complete prescription for success for another person's life. In our case, the basic principles of *Baby Wise* were a great starting-point for our family. They are as follows:

1. Plan feedings approximately every three hours.
2. Feed your babies soon after they wake up, and then try to keep them awake for a while thereafter, so that their routine is Feed/Awake-time/Sleep...Feed/Awake-time/Sleep.

---

15 Ezzo, Gary, and Robert Bucknam. On Becoming Baby Wise: Giving Your Infant the Gift of Nighttime Sleep. Louisiana, Missouri: Parent-Wise Solutions, 2001.

3. Try not to let babies become overly dependent on any sleep prop, including eating immediately before sleeping.
4. Generally work towards having your babies' needs fit into the needs of the family, rather than creating a completely child-centered household.

This Feed/Awake-time/Sleep routine is fully explained in *Baby Wise*, complete with the philosophy and research behind this routine, and it promises that an amazingly high percentage of babies who follow this practice will sleep through the night by around seven weeks—and their awake time will be happier, too. I have no doubt that our girls would have slept through the night by seven weeks if our pediatrician hadn't directed us to keep feeding our preemies around the clock for an extended period of time. As it was, our girls started to sleep through the night as soon as our pediatrician gave us the green light to try it. (By the way, a pediatrician's definition of "through the night" generally means six hours—not the twelve hours through the night that they'll get to later—but six hours straight seems miraculous when you're used to feeding babies every three hours in the middle of the night.)

Why Feed/Awake-time/Sleep? You have probably seen or at least heard of babies being fed and lulled to sleep by the comforts of nursing or suckling a bottle, even being put to bed with bottles, and nodding off with full tummies. Besides what Ezzo and Bucknam point out in *Baby Wise*, here are some reasons you specifically do **not** want to fall into the habit of Awake-time/Feed/Sleep with twins:

1. The easier it is to get your babies to fall asleep, the happier you'll be. In the short-run, it is sometimes easier to get babies to fall asleep while eating, but in the long-run, you'll have two babies who are dependent on being fed in order to fall asleep. Picture this: It's the end of the day, you're exhausted, your babies are cranky and tired, but they won't fall asleep without a bottle or breast. If you feed them separately, you have one fussy baby waiting while you're trying to hurry the other one through his feeding, and then you have to deftly move the first sleeping baby to the crib without waking him before repeating with the second baby. If you feed them simultaneously, you have the delicate job of getting two sleeping babies off the boobs and transported to bed without waking them. I know there are moms who do it this way, but I preferred laying them in their crib awake and having them learn the life skill of falling asleep on their own. Did I feed them to sleep from time to time? Umm, yeah... Desperate times call for desperate measures. But generally speaking, the mission was to have them fall asleep without the crutch of feeding them to sleep. The earlier they are taught to self-soothe without eating, the easier your life will be—and they can learn to do this very early if you start them on a Feed/Awake-time/Sleep cycle in the weeks just after they're born.

2. If you have your babies' awake time first, and then you feed them, you will be rolling the dice about when meal time will be—and you could very likely have two screaming, hungry, mad babies on your hands, demanding to be fed at the same time. Just the thought of it makes me shudder. Yes, you can begin to anticipate when they're starting to get hungry and do your best to feed them before they become really serious about it, but it'll be a guessing game. On the other hand, if you set the precedent that they eat when you wake them up, you are much more in control. As they're approaching hunger, they'll be sleeping. Their awake time will be happier when they're not getting hungry and cranky. And while they won't be lulled to sleep by completely full bellies, they will still be full enough to fall asleep comfortably.

Yes, your babies may eat more often than on the three-hour schedule in their first couple of weeks. But when they become accustomed to your waking them at certain times and eating at certain times, they will learn to be hungry at those times, and they will soon predictably wake up on their own at those times. If you've ever had a scheduled lunch break, you know that when Saturday rolls around, you are still hungry for lunch at about the same time— your body becomes programmed to being hungry at the time that you normally eat. It works the same way with scheduling your babies' feedings. You're not depriving them food when they're hungry; they actually become predictably hungry at the times that they're accustomed to eating. What's more, your body can more reliably produce enough milk for two when it knows that every X hours, it's baby chow time. (Unfortunately, unlike adults, they will not "sleep in" just because it's Saturday...the idea is to keep them from becoming sleep-deprived like working adults who crave extra sleep on the weekends...but the analogy about getting hungry does apply.)

We read *Baby Wise* and thought, "Okay! We like the idea of having a predictable routine! We like the idea of them not (often) screaming for food at the same time! And we really like the idea of them sleeping through the night sooner than later! ...But how will we do it with two?" Hopefully, this chapter will help you adapt the aforementioned principles into your family's routine.

What time do you want to get up?

I decided early-on that it would work well for us if the girls were on a 7am - 10am - 1pm - 4pm - 7pm...feeding schedule. I figured that if they were eating every three hours (which they were doing 24/7 for two months and during the day until they were almost five months old), a 6 - 9 - 12 - 3 schedule would have me getting up earlier in the morning than I personally care to, and an 8 - 11 - 2 - 5 schedule would have me going to bed later than I wanted to—if they each nursed for half an hour starting at 11pm, it would be after midnight before I could go to bed. 7 - 10 - 1 - 4 seemed like the best compromise for me. Plus, eventually, I hoped the girls would sleep 7pm to 7am, which would give us an opportunity to eat dinner at a reasonable hour after we put them to bed—or enjoy a meal as a family before bedtime as they got older—and still have a couple of hours of "grown-up time" before we needed to go to bed ourselves

Yes, I said if they nursed for half an hour—each. As you may have read in the chapter on breastfeeding, I am a big proponent of breastfeeding. However, it didn't work well for me to feed them simultaneously. I was determined to breastfeed, however, so I fed them back-to-back. Was this extremely time-consuming? Yes. Was it worth it? Definitely. I firmly believe in the long-term health benefits of breastfeeding and was able to witness the near-term benefits as my preemies, born in the winter in Oklahoma, did not have as much as a cold until they were nine months old. {But again, in case you skipped the chapter on breastfeeding, no judgment here if you decide that breastfeeding is not for you. Having a sane mama is more important to your babies' welfare than breastmilk!}

The sample schedules below are based on nursing babies back-to-back; if you can do it simultaneously, awesome! That will buy you a lot of time. If you nurse simultaneously or bottle-feed your babies, it should be easy enough to adjust the following schedules to match your family's needs.

But I've always heard, "Never Wake a Sleeping Baby..."

Babies are not born knowing when to sleep and when to be awake—most parents will tell you that their newborns had their days and nights "mixed up" for a while. I've heard it said that this is due to mom's movements during the day lulling her unborn babies to sleep, making them more active at night—a pattern that continues for a while after birth. By waking your babies when they're supposed to be awake, they'll be sleepier when it's time to sleep, and you'll teach them when to be awake and when to be asleep—which is when you want to be asleep, too!

Example Schedules

In the following pages are some example schedules that worked for our family. As with all things in this book, **this is meant to be a starting-point for you**; this exact routine may not work for you and your family, but hopefully it will give you a place to start. When we were expecting our girls/had newborns and were trying to figure out a routine, all I could find were vague schedules and really wanted something specific to go by—hopefully, even though this may be overly detailed, it will be helpful to you.

You'll notice "Baby A" and "Baby B"—I alternated who nursed first each day to try to keep things as equitable as possible, and I found it very helpful for the first several weeks to have a notebook on their changing table where I kept track of who ate at what time, who had poopy diapers when, and so forth. (See Appendix—there are great apps for this now, too.) I know that it sounds neurotic, but in the beginning I could barely tell who was who—much less could I remember who had eaten first that day, who had nursed on which side, or who had pooped eight times or not at all in the last 24 hours. (Your pediatrician will ask about those poops when you go in for well-baby visits, and he will ask for even more details about the frequency, color, and consistency of your babies' bowel movements if they get sick or start to have any health problems.) Sleep deprivation for a new mommy of twins is pretty rough—writing things down was the only way I could remember a thing.

Newborn to Two Months

Feedings every three hours around the clock! (based on the advice of our pediatrician)

7:00 am	Wake Baby A and nurse.
7:30 am	Hand Baby A to Daddy or a visitor, or place Baby A in a bouncy seat. Wake Baby B and nurse. If someone else was available, I'd ask them to burp Baby A so I could go ahead and get started with Baby B a little early.
	"Playtime"—also time to change diapers as needed. We discovered after a while that they were happiest if they could eat immediately after waking instead of being tortured with a cold diaper change right away. Plus, they're likely to poop during or after eating, so a diaper change before that is just adding to the already huge number of diapers you have to change/buy/wash.
8:30 am	Put Baby A down for a nap. Continue awake time with Baby B.
9:00 am	Put Baby B down for a nap—by staggering their schedules, each will get 1 ½-hour naps. If you can feed simultaneously and get them to sleep simultaneously, even better.
9:00 am - 10:00 am	Both babies sleeping. You really should sleep, too. Really.
10:00 am	Wake Baby A and repeat three-hour routine as above, staggering feeding/napping schedules by 30 minutes.
1:00 pm	Wake Baby A and repeat three-hour routine as above, staggering feeding/napping schedules by 30 minutes.
4:00 pm	Wake Baby A and nurse.

4:30 pm	Wake Baby B and nurse.
	During this awake time, give the babies their baths in anticipation of bedtime. Dress them in their pajamas, as this next naptime will eventually become bedtime. The sooner you start a bedtime routine, the better.
5:30 pm	Put Baby A down for a nap.*
6:00 pm	Put Baby B down for a nap.
6:00 pm - 7:00 pm	Both babies sleeping…*OR you might try keeping the babies awake until the 7:00 feeding, after which they'll go to bed "for the night." You'll probably need to go ahead and let them have this nap, too, though, especially in the first weeks.
7:00 pm	Wake Baby A, nurse, change diaper, and put back to bed as soon as possible, beginning the pattern for 7:00 bedtime.
7:30 pm	Wake Baby B, nurse, change diaper, and put back to bed as soon as possible.
10:00 pm	Wake Baby A, nurse, change diaper, and put back to bed as soon as possible. Repeat with Baby B.
1:00 am	Repeat nighttime feeding routine.
4:00 am	Repeat nighttime feeding routine.

Won't they wake each other up?

No. Newborn babies are good at sleeping soundly—it's one of the things they do best! Their bodies are desperate for rest, because all of that rapid growth takes a lot of energy. There is no need to tip-toe around most newborns, and the longer they go without people trying to keep quiet while they're sleeping, the longer they'll be able to sleep with Dad cooking in the kitchen, Mom vacuuming in the nursery, or Twin Sister crying in the same crib. For most babies, honeymoon period of sleep oblivion ends around six months, when they start becoming much more aware of the world around them. In the meantime, enjoy their ability to sleep through most anything.

Adding the use of a breast pump to the feeding schedule

For a while, our girls were unable to nurse because they were born before their suck-swallow reflexes kicked in. In the meantime, I pumped breast milk to bottle-feed them. During this time, I would pump shortly after putting Baby B down for her nap. It would take about 20 minutes with a double electric pump, and I didn't want to cut it too close to Baby A waking up again for fear of being stuck to the pump with a crying baby and/or not having adequate milk ready when I had a hungry baby to feed. When someone else was around, I'd wake the girls at the same time and have the other person feed one baby a bottle—then they'd both sleep at the same time, buying a little more time for Mommy. At night, I/we'd bottle feed them, and then I'd pump before going back to sleep. Not much sleep for Mommy, and because my husband is a pilot, I took most of the night shift because he needed his sleep to be safe in the cockpit. Thank goodness for our DVR so I could watch Oprah or Friends re-runs at 1:00 or 4:00 am to keep me awake if I needed to!

When the girls learned to nurse at about one month, I continued pumping about half the time so I could alternate breast and bottle at our pediatrician's advice (see the chapter on breastfeeding). When I was both nursing and pumping, I would nurse at one feeding, then pump for the next feeding while they were napping, as close to their waking time as I dared to cut it so my body would be on a three-hour feeding schedule, ready to nurse at the next feeding.

Putting babies to sleep

We tried to keep our bedtime routine as simple as possible, while still providing some bedtime cues. For example, they had a bath every night just before bedtime, and we played a quiet CD of some sort in the background while they were falling asleep, but we did not create an elaborate, complicated, long routine of rocking, singing, reading books, and so forth. It seemed to us that a simpler routine would get them to sleep sooner, give us some much-needed grown-

...nd make it easier for them to a babysitter, if we were traveling, ...ed sometimes; no, it was not easy ...es, it took some work, but our ...rsistence paid off.

Throug... the combined advice of our pediatrician and something we read somewhere, we found that the best, fastest, easiest way to get our girls to go to sleep was to lay them in their crib(s) at the time we had determined as naptime/bedtime. We would swaddle them (hospital nursery nurses are great coaches for this skill), and lay them on their backs (the safest way to sleep according to the American Academy of Pediatrics at that time). If they were wide awake, fine; if they were drowsy, fine. We drove ourselves crazy for a while trying to get them drowsy before putting them to bed in the evenings, which was an exhausting and frustrating waste of time. Also beware that if you let them get too tired before putting them down, they can get overly tired and fussy and have difficulty falling asleep. I've experienced this myself from time to time—being so exhausted that it's hard to fall asleep. It's best to just put your babies to bed when you know they need to sleep.

Our girls were never rocked to sleep, so they did not learn that they could only fall asleep when rocked. If you start simply laying them in the cribs when it's time to sleep early on, they will never know the difference, and they will teach themselves how to fall asleep. I loved the romantic notion of rocking a baby to sleep, but babies quickly become dependent on that, and as a parent of twins, you don't have time in the day to add another task to your to-do list. There's plenty of other time to snuggle those sweet babies!

Once this routine was established, our girls began to wake every three hours during the day without us having to wake them.

Two to Four Months

At about two months (two weeks gestational age), we were given the green light to let the girls sleep four or five hours at a stretch at

night. Let me tell you, after an exhausting two mon'
them every three hours around the clock, that was like
over again. Our daytime schedule was the same, but I ..
(and me!) sleep longer at night. I still fed them at about 10:00 pm ..
their late evening feeding, since I was basically up anyway, and then
I would only need to feed them once in the middle of the night
before they woke up again at 7:00 am. Since I was afraid they'd
sleep all night and not get the nutrition their preemie bodies needed,
I'd set an alarm for something like 3:00 am, but if they woke up
before that I'd go ahead and nurse them then. If one baby woke up,
the other one would get fed and changed right after I put the first one
back to bed. This helped to cut back on the number of times I'd have
to wake up, and it helped with keeping them on the same schedule.

At about three months (six weeks gestational age), we were told
that we could let them try to sleep through the night. They would
still get a late evening feeding right before I went to bed (at about
10:00), but it was our goal for them to sleep until morning after that
feeding. The first time one of them did that, I was singing "All Night
Long!" by Lionel Ritchie the whole next day. Yes, I'm cool like that.
It did not happen every night, and often one would sleep through the
night and the other wouldn't; it took a while before both of them
were sleeping through the night on a regular basis, but what an
improvement over responding to alarms in the middle of the night!
Once we were aiming to have them sleep through the night, if they
did wake up I would try not to nurse them unless I became
desperate—nursing was a sure-fire way to get them to fall back
asleep, but I didn't want them to stay hooked on that middle-of-the-
night meal—and I stopped waking one just because the other one
woke up.

Four to Eight Months

At about five months (3 ½ months gestational age), we were told
they could go four hours between daytime feedings. I felt like I was
given my freedom! As you can imagine, it's nearly impossible to do
anything besides feed and diaper babies when they have to eat every
three hours. Since we were continuing with the Feed/Awake-time/
Sleep routine, changing their feeding schedule effectively changed
their sleep schedule. It was at about the same time that we decided to
try dropping the late evening feeding, which we had gradually

oved earlier—to about 9:00. Also, by around seven months they started receiving more calories from solids than from breast milk, and they were more efficient and stronger at nursing, so nursing time gradually decreased from 30 minutes per baby to 10-15 minutes per baby. Their new routine came to look something like this:

7:00 am	Wake and nurse Baby A. By this time, they woke up on their own—if they slept late I counted my blessings! (If they both woke up, Baby B would have to wait in her crib, bouncy seat, or lying/sitting/playing on the floor.)
7:20 am	Nurse Baby B.
7:45 am - 9:30 am	Solid food breakfast in high chairs and then playtime. At about six months, we started introducing "solid" foods. (How one part rice cereal and four parts breast milk or formula is considered "solid" is beyond me.) It took a while to work up to three meals a day with solid foods, but by the time they were eight months old, they were doing that. Breakfast came immediately after both had been nursed.
9:30 am - 11:00 am	Naptime. Sometime during this period, they started waking each other up, and I stopped trying to stagger naps.
11:00 am	Wake and nurse Baby A.
11:20 am	Nurse Baby B.
11:45am - 1:30 pm	Lunchtime and playtime—lunch immediately followed nursing.
1:30 pm - 3:00 pm	Naptime
3:00 pm	Wake and nurse Baby A.

3:20 pm	Wake and nurse Baby B.
3:40 pm - 4:30 pm	Playtime
4:30 pm - 5:00-ish	Naptime—catnap
5:00-ish	Nurse Baby A.
5:20 pm	Nurse Baby B.
6:00 pm	Dinnertime, then bath time
7:00 pm	Bedtime

Nine to Twelve Months

By the time the girls were eight months old, their naps were getting shorter and shorter—sometimes as short as 30 minutes. This allowed more time for meals and such, but they were crankier, and I was worried that they weren't getting adequate rest. I was talking about this to my friend, Melanie, and she said, "Maybe it's time for them to go down to two naps a day." Oh. I guess we had been cruising along with a routine that worked—or sort-of worked—and it hadn't dawned on me to change it. One thing I quickly learned about motherhood—just when you think you have everything figured out, things change, especially in that first year when their developmental needs change so rapidly. So I tried taking the girls down to two naps a day, and they almost immediately adjusted with wonderful results—they stayed asleep longer (1½- to 2-hour naps) and were happier because of it. Plus, my life became easier when I was only trying to squeeze things I needed to do out of the house around two naps instead of three. Unless it was something really important, it just wasn't worth it to me to mess with their naps. At this point, they were getting most of their calories from solids and only nursed about ten minutes apiece at each feeding. Then their schedule looked something like this:

7:00-ish am	Wake and nurse Baby A. (They would almost always wake up on their own by this time, and one would bide her time playing on the floor or visiting with Daddy while her sister nursed.)
7:15 am	Nurse Baby B.
7:30 am - 10:00 am	Breakfast in their high chairs, and then playtime.
10:00 am - 11:30 am	Naptime
11:30 am - 12:00 pm	Wake and nurse babies.
12:00 pm - 2:00 pm	Lunch in high chairs, and then playtime. This became the most likely time of day for me to take them on errands.
2:00 pm - 2:30 pm	Nurse Baby A and then Baby B. (By this age, I was not as concerned about nursing them right before a nap, and it was the best way to fit another nursing session in the day with only two naps.)
2:30 pm - 4:30 pm	Naptime
4:30 pm - 5:30 pm	Playtime
5:30 pm	Nurse Baby A and then Baby B.
6:00 pm	Dinner in high chairs, followed by bathtime.
7:00 pm	Bedtime

One Year and Beyond...

I started weaning the girls at about one year, gradually dropping feedings until the last one was gone. (First I dropped the lunch feeding, then the afternoon feeding, then the dinner feeding, and finally the morning feeding.) I fed them cow's milk from sippy cups with their meals, and then their routine was this:

7:00-ish am	Wake up and get in high chairs for breakfast. (They wanted to eat right away!)
	Playtime
10:00 am - 11:30 am	Naptime
11:30 am	Wake up and get in high chairs for lunch.
	Playtime
2:30 pm - 4:00 pm	Naptime
4:00 pm	Wake up and get in high chairs for a snack.
	Playtime
5:30 pm	Dinnertime in high chairs
6:30 pm	Bathtime
7:00 pm	Bedtime

The Last Nap Schedule

At around 13 months, I started noticing the same thing I'd noticed when they were ready to go from three naps to two: Their naps were getting shorter, and sometimes they wouldn't nap at all. Once again, I went to the books and to Melanie—the books said that toddlers usually drop their second nap at about 18 months, but Melanie said one of her daughters waited that long, and the other was ready to go to one nap at about 12 months. I think one of my girls might have held onto that second nap a while longer, but there was no way I was going to try to have them on different schedules. So at about 13 months we dropped the second nap, and they went to taking one 2- to 3-hour nap a day within a couple of weeks. Not only were they getting more rest again, I had even more freedom—longer spans of wake-time to run errands, go to church on Sundays, etc., and a much longer block of naptime to get things done, rest a bit, and so on. You'll notice lots of "–ishes" in there—the older they are, the easier it is to be flexible. Here's what their toddler schedule looked like:

7:00-ish am	Wake up and get in high chairs for breakfast.
	Playtime
11:00 am	Lunch in high chairs
12:00-ish pm - 3:00-ish pm	Naptime
3:00 pm	Playtime with a snack around 3:00 or 3:30
5:00-ish pm	Dinner in high chairs
6:00-ish pm	Bathtime
6:30 pm - 7:00 pm	Bedtime

When the Going Gets Tough

Was it ever difficult to establish and maintain this schedule? Oh my goodness, YES! Especially if you find yourself with two colicky babies, you may need to have them sleep in swings or vibrating bouncy seats for a few weeks, feed them more frequently, whatever it takes to soothe them and keep your wits about you until the colic passes, usually by about three months. (Search "colic twins" online for a multitude of ideas on coping with colic.)

Our girls were fed via feeding tubes for the first eight days of their lives. While we were thankful that they were healthy—just in need of a little more time to grow and develop—it was obviously painful for new parents to see their precious babies hooked up to tubes and machines, unable to leave their incubators for more than a few minutes at a time. A silver lining to their time in the NICU, though, was that they ate every three hours—no more, no less—from day one. I never asked myself, "Is she crying because she's hungry? Maybe I should feed her even though it's only been an hour… Did she eat enough? Maybe I should try to feed her some more…" When we transitioned the girls from feeding tubes to bottles (under the direction of the NICU nurses), they had a bottle exactly every three hours. And so, even though feeding them was very difficult for the first month, as we were constantly challenged by transitioning them from feeding tubes to bottles to breast (see the breastfeeding chapter for more details), at least their appetites had already been regulated to the three-hour routine that we were hoping to create.

I guess you can take from my experience, "Gee, Susanna sure was lucky to have those NICU nurses establish a feeding schedule early on," OR you might think, "Well, if the people whose profession it is to grow healthy, strong babies think that feeding them every three hours works, then I'll stick with that, too." If you do find yourself in the new mom quandary of trying to balance your desire to establish a schedule with meeting the needs of a crying baby who seems hungry off-schedule, only you in that moment can decide the best course of action. If you are convinced that your baby needs to eat, feed him! But realize that if you make a habit of feeding your babies outside of desired mealtimes, you are prolonging the time until you have them in a predictable, Mommy-directed—and thereby less stressful for everyone—routine.

While we tried to always have our girls sleep in their crib(s), we did find ourselves going through spells when one wouldn't nap in the crib for whatever reason. I'd want to pull my hair out, but in the name of maintaining my sanity and ensuring our girls were getting adequate rest, I'd put one baby in a Pack-n-Play in the master bedroom or let her doze in the swing for a nap or two—or ten—and then work on getting both babies napping in the crib again. You will occasionally have to "break the rules" to keep them on track—or get them back on track—and sleeping at the times that you know are in their best interest. I'd much rather have a baby take a nap in a swing, but get the sleep he needs and keep his body accustomed to a nap at a given time of day, than to skip the nap entirely. Sometimes our girls did skip naps entirely for a day or for several days on end, but my husband and I always went back to Plan A—naps and feedings on a schedule, sleeping in the crib—and with diligence and patience, the girls went back to Plan A with us. I even remember a couple of times that one of the girls wouldn't fall asleep at night, and so we put a Pack-n-Play in our laundry room—as far away from the bedrooms as possible—so she could cry it out and not keep her sister and daddy awake. Yes, I checked on her every few minutes and tried to soothe her, yes it was painful for Mommy to listen to her cry, but yes, she did eventually fall asleep.

Moms whose babies have been on a fairly strict feeding and sleeping schedule will tell you that these instances were the exception rather than the rule. Bumps in the road happen to *all* parents. Just keep in mind that establishing a regular routine takes *time, consistency,* and *patience.* You will almost certainly not have your babies in a perfectly predictable three-hour routine when they are two weeks old...and maybe not even when they are two months old. The idea is to be as consistent as you can and get them trending in the right direction. Bend but don't break. It takes a little while to get there—a little while that can seem like an eternity when you're in the middle of it—but with time, consistency, and patience, you will have a highly predictable routine and well-rested, happier babies.

Final Comments about Sleep and Routines

While it's important to notice their changing sleep needs and adjust accordingly, do not jump the gun—it's very common for babies and young children to go through phases for a few days or a week or two, and then revert to "normal." At 3 ½ years old, our girls still took a 1 ½ -hour nap almost every day—and even when they didn't sleep, they rested in their beds for that amount of time. Every so often during their toddler/preschool years, we'd have several days or a couple of weeks where their naps were

Don't give up on their naps!

hit-or-miss, but I'm so glad we didn't give up on their naps! I think that most of the times that children under about the age of three "give up their naps," it's more the parents who have given up than the children. Children still need some daytime sleep *and* a 12-hour night's rest for healthy development until *at least* age three (many still need naps until about age five)[16], and will continue to need 11-12 hours of sleep at night for years thereafter. Our girls kept going back to their naps and were much happier—and so was I—when they'd had some rest in the middle of the day.

Also realize that it will usually take a whole week—maybe more like ten days to two weeks—to determine whether or not a new feeding or sleeping routine is working for your babies. If your pediatrician tells you it's time to drop a feeding or you sense that it's time for them to take two naps a day instead of three, don't give up if the first few days on your new schedule are a disaster. Know that it will take a while for your babies to adjust and adapt to the change—think of how you feel if you're jet-lagged. Try to stick with it for at least a week or two, and if after two weeks things still aren't working out, then it's time to reevaluate.

Yes, they really do need that much sleep! It really struck me in my first trimester how surprisingly tired I was. Growing (two tiny babies in that case) takes a lot of energy, and your babies will grow by leaps and bounds that first year—and for years thereafter. Make sure they get the rest they need to grow healthy and strong! They—and you—will be so much happier for it.

---

[16] Children and Sleep - National Sleep Foundation. (n.d.). Retrieved October 24, 2016, from https://sleepfoundation.org/sleep-topics/children-and-sleep/page/0/2

•8•

...And They're Off!

Solid Foods, Going Out,

and Changes with Growing Babies

It seemed that for the first six months of our girls' lives, they were pretty much the same. Yes, they began smiling and laughing, they went from nursing every three hours around the clock to nursing four times a day and sleeping through the night, and we marveled at their ability to grasp a toy and shake it with delight. Otherwise, though, they stayed pretty much the same—and by the same, I mean they stayed in the same place. At around six months, though, the girls began to change dramatically and at a rapid pace. Off to the races!

Introducing Solid Foods

Many books say that you can begin introducing solid foods to babies between four and six months of age. I was in no hurry to do this, partly on the advice of our pediatrician and partly on the advice of a friend who has a little girl a few months older than ours. I remember her saying when her daughter was about four months old, "We just started feeding her solids—I don't know why I was in such a hurry to do that! It was so much easier when she only drank her meals!"

At our daughters' well-baby appointment at around four months (we had been out of town at three months, and our pediatrician had given us the okay to wait), the girls were still nursing exclusively, and our pediatrician said that we didn't need to start them on solids for at least a few more weeks—as long as they seemed to get enough to eat, we should continue nursing exclusively, but we would probably notice within the next several weeks that they would stop being able to sleep through the night on breast milk alone, which would signal us that it was time to introduce solids. Sure enough—about six weeks later, we had several nights in a row during which the girls woke up hungry in the night. So that Saturday evening, when my husband was home and able to help, we mixed some rice cereal—about 1 tablespoon of cereal with a lot of breast milk—strapped the girls into their papasan chairs, and "spoon-fed" them for the first time. We oohed and ahhed, recorded the event on video and still pictures, and were very proud of their first attempt at eating "solid" food. They got it all over their little faces, but weren't they cute? And so grown up! We could hardly believe our babies were eating from a spoon.

The next time I sat down to feed them in their little chairs, it was still endearing to me that they were getting food all over their faces, that more liquidy rice cereal dribbled out of their mouths than actually made it into their little bodies, that their little hands would occasionally bat the spoon away just as I neared their mouths... Sometimes they would open their little mouths for the spoon, but a lot of the time I'd have to sort-of pry their mouths open, or they'd have their tongues in the way of getting any food, but that was okay—they were just learning. They were just beginning to be developmentally ready for this new chapter in their little lives. Cute, right?

But after a few meals spent this way, I became frustrated. I knew that this was just practice, that their nutritional needs were still mostly being met through nursing, but come on! Thirty minutes nursing one baby, thirty minutes nursing the other baby, five minutes preparing cereal, thirty minutes "feeding" cereal to them, five minutes cleaning babies and their bowl and spoon...as they improve at eating this way and I worked them up to "eating" three meals a day this way, I was spending about an hour and 40 minutes at each feeding, plus another hour for a fourth feeding that was only nursing...That was **six hours a day** that I was spending just feeding them! Plus, they were still napping with every feeding cycle...1 ½ hours feeding...1 ½ hours napping...That didn't leave much time for playtime, or reading books, or going for walks, or anything! A couple of weeks into this new routine, I was going crazy. And the worst part was that spoon-feeding felt like the greatest exercise in futility of my life. Sometimes, they would eat like champs; other times I felt like we were starting over at square one. I was sure that they would eventually get better at this—I mean, no kid goes to kindergarten unable to eat from a spoon—but I was growing impatient. And when they both discovered "blowing raspberries" while eating, that having food in their mouths made that sound even more fun, I was amused for about two seconds before I wanted to scream.

It was at this point that I began seriously considering weaning them. Spending six hours a day feeding them was wearing me out, and I was worried that they weren't getting enough time to do other things. Their tummies were a little sensitive, so I had to be careful not to give them "tummy time" right after a meal or they would spit up quite a bit, which put additional limits on their non-meal/non-nap time. I talked to my husband, friends, and my mom about weaning them. Everyone was very supportive of whatever I felt was best— after all, I had done a great service to them to nurse them for this long; most babies in this day and age aren't breastfed for so many months, and to do it with twins was really going above and beyond. I had always had in mind that I would nurse them until they were about six or seven months old, and we were there, so it must be time, right?

So what was my hesitation? I knew that they would be fine on formula—almost every child I knew had been formula-fed for some or most of their infancy, and they were all just fine. But it just didn't feel right to me. It made me get teary-eyed to think of weaning them, and it gave me a terrible feeling in the pit of my stomach. Was I just emotionally tied to nursing them? It had taken so long to get them to nurse in the first place—was that the reason I was reluctant to give it up? It would certainly be less of a drain on my time and my body if I ottles. But it would also be expensive. But that wasn't as ⟨...⟩ my time and my health and what would give them the ⟨...⟩ of nutrition and time to do other things. Plus we had a long road trip coming up, and it would be a lot easier to feed them bottles than to nurse them along the way. What to do, what to do...

Just when I had almost convinced myself to wean them, we turned a corner. The girls seemed to suddenly become more proficient at eating their rice cereal and the few pureed veggies and fruits we had introduced, and when that happened, they stopped needing quite as much breast milk. I also believe they became even more efficient nursers at this point, the result being that instead of each needing to nurse for thirty minutes at each feeding, they began nursing for only about ten minutes each. At first I was concerned that they weren't getting enough breast milk, but then I realized (along with some assurance from our pediatrician) that their nutritional and hydration needs were being met. Yes!

> At around six months, the time your babies spend nursing each day will decrease, making it easier to continue nursing.

After a little while, feeding them became manageable again. And I wasn't frustrated with their inability to spoon-feed—they had finally gotten rather good at it. Now, when reassessing our situation, I realized that it would probably take as long or longer to prepare bottles, feed them with bottles, and wash bottles, as it was taking to nurse them for ten minutes each at each feeding. And I did want to keep nursing them. I wanted them to have the health benefits of breast milk for as long as possible, at least until they were a year old and could drink cow's milk (as recommended by the American Academy of Pediatrics). Whew!

Some tips on feeding solids to twins:
(Consult your pediatrician on what is best for your babies' needs.)

- Start with baby rice cereal: 1 part cereal to about 3-4 parts breast milk or formula. It will taste mostly like milk to them, will be very runny, and will make a big mess. They need to ease into the texture of "solids," though, and will do best spoon-feeding with a familiar taste/texture. Start with one meal a day, gradually thickening it, and gradually adding additional feedings.

*A side note: Baby rice cereal tends to continue to dissolve in breast milk, so if you make it the consistency you want before the meal, it'll end up pretty watery by the time your babies are finished. And I found that adding dry cereal after the fact is likely to make the mixture lumpy. In other words, you might want to make it just a little thicker than the desired consistency, knowing that it'll thin out as you feed it to your babies.

* Another side note: Babies don't seem to care whether their food is cold or hot, so do you yourself a favor and don't bother heating their food. They'll develop a taste for hot and cold later—no need to create extra work for yourself now!

• I know most health professionals would balk at this, but I recommend using one bowl and one spoon to feed them. It is so much easier to just feed one bite to one, one bite to the next, and alternate back and forth that way without having to switch spoons and bowls. Just make double the portion in one bowl and save yourself some time and trouble. I mean, do you really think that after sharing a room and a bed and toys and putting their hands in each other's mouths that sharing a spoon will be the thing that will cause them to catch each other's colds? I guess it might be worth the trouble if you know that one is really sick, but I figure that it's nearly impossible to keep them from sharing germs. (And mine never got as much as a cold until they were nine months old!)

Why bother with separate spoons?

- After they've gotten the hang of cereal, introduce pureed vegetables, one at a time, several days to a week or so apart so you can monitor for food allergies. I used jarred baby foods at first, and then when they showed that they liked something, I would cook it and puree it myself. I liked saving a little money this way and knowing exactly what was going into my babies' little bodies. (You might like to have one of those mini food processors for this stage. I wore one out!) We tried carrots first, which they did not like—sweet potatoes would have been a better first "yellow" vegetable for my girls' tastes. And when we moved on to greens, we tried sweet peas first, thinking they would be sweet and yummy, but they hated them. Green beans, sweet potatoes, and squash were their first favorites.
- Next, introduce fruits in a similar manner. I've heard it said that if you introduce fruits first, they won't get a taste for veggies because they prefer the fruits' sweet taste. The first fruit we tried were bananas, which they didn't particularly like—and when I tasted the baby food bananas, I thought they tasted weird, too. They did like apple sauce and pears, and they later liked bananas when I pureed fresh ones myself.
- If one or both of your babies doesn't like a veggie or fruit, try it again after a few days or a couple of weeks. Sometimes they grow to like something when it becomes more familiar to them. Also, you might try mixing some of an unliked food in with something they do like—carrots were a big one for us. They hated them alone, but had no problem with some mixed in with their squash or sweet potatoes. There was no hope for strained peas, though—sometimes you just have move on.
- I read somewhere to work up to the following daily menu. It worked really well for us.

Breakfast: breast milk (or formula), 1 cereal and 1 fruit
Lunch: breast milk (or formula), 1 fruit and 1 vegetable
Snack: breast milk (or formula)
Dinner: breast milk (or formula), 1 cereal and 1 vegetable

I would always try to include one green vegetable each day, and I eventually used baby oatmeal cereal for breakfast and baby rice cereal for dinner. Our girls grew to prefer veggies and fruits to their cereal, so after a while, I just mixed the

prepared cereal with a veggie or fruit to make it r
to them. Those baby cereals are such a good sou
it is recommended to give at least one serving of the
until they are a year old.

- Buyer, beware: Read baby food labels carefully. I was shocked
  to see how many prepared baby foods have sugar in them—
  definitely not something babies need—and when they got older
  and started eating chunkier foods, I couldn't believe how many
  toddler foods have a huge amount of sodium in them. One
  boasted of having no preservatives, but had enough salt to
  mummify a cat—I compared a serving of that toddler food to
  an adult serving of potato chips, and the baby food had more
  sodium! Yikes!

Out-and-About with Two Babies

Because our girls were preemies and were born at the beginning
of cold & flu season, I did not take them anywhere for quite a while.
Our pediatrician and the doctors at the hospital scared us silly about
the risks that respiratory syncytial virus (RSV), the flu, pneumonia,
and even the common cold can pose to preemies, and we didn't take
any chances. I grocery shopped after my husband got home from
work and on the weekends, or I asked him to pick things up on his
way home. We even took turns going to church. However, before
you know it you will need to and be able to go places—or you may
have older children or other motivation to get out of the house
sooner than I did—so here are some tips on getting out-and-about:

- Keep your stroller in your car and use it! Try to buy one that
  will accommodate *two* infant car seat carriers. Try it out in the
  store before you buy to make sure it'll work. I think I carried
  both infant carriers in my arms into their first pediatrician's
  appointment, and that was the only time I attempted that
  maneuver—carrying two of those things is just too
  cumbersome.
- Load and unload babies to/from their infant seats in the
  comfort of your home. Get them dressed, changed, buckled in
  (and bundled up in cold weather) inside the house, and then
  take the seats out to the car to quickly pop them in their bases,
  and then go.

- If you're grocery shopping, you can take the stroller in the store *and* push a shopping cart—this *can* be done. If you try to forego the stroller, you may have to push two carts anyway—one with the car seat carriers and one with groceries, or one infant carrier per cart. At least if you use your stroller you have the benefit of being able to load them into the stroller at your car. You will attract a LOT of attention doing this. Smile when people ask you questions, like "Are they twins???"
- OR you can carry one infant in a BabyBjorn or other baby carrier, and put the other baby in an infant seat in the grocery cart. Or carry them both in a TwinGo carrier, made for two.
- When they are able to sit up, you can put them in one grocery cart together. Seat them so they're facing each other in the baby seat part of the shopping cart, each with one leg through a leg hole and the other leg propped up in the seat. This one's a real crowd-pleaser—you'll get a lot of "Oh my gosh! They're SO cute!" (When they start sitting in the cart, you might want one of those grocery cart covers to go in it.)

Julie-Rose's babies, shopping with Mommy

- The Buggy Bench is a new product, designed by a mother of twins, that straps to the shopping cart behind the existing seat, creating an additional seat for child number two. You can find it at http://www.buggybench.com/
- If you're not using your stroller, park as close to a cart corral in the parking lot as you can, so you can get the cart, bring it to your car, and load the kiddos directly into it. And then you can also unload them back into the car and return the cart without leaving sight of your babies.
- When shopping in general, you'll want a tandem stroller rather than a side-by-side. A side-by-side is really difficult to navigate through narrow, crowded stores.

- After they outgrow sitting in the baby seat part of the cart together, pushing two carts is doable, but tou~~~~ don't see a special cart built with two seats, a~~~~ ~~~~many grocery stores, Wal-Mart, Target, etc. have them, but they may be tucked out of sight.
- When they're old enough for snacks, always plan for them to have a snack while you're shopping. It'll keep them busy and happy. Munchkin makes a great Snack-Catcher for snacking on the go.

Set Them Up for Success

Another golden nugget from my friend, Melanie, was to "set them up for success." We've all been to Wal-Mart at 9:00 at night and seen (and heard) a screaming two-year-old and thought to ourselves, "Why isn't that child in bed?" I know there are times that it can't be avoided, but if at all possible, set your children up for success. If taking them to a company picnic means they'll miss their nap, you may be setting yourself and your babies (and everyone there) up for a miserable afternoon. It may be better to miss an event than to grace everyone's presence with a pair of cranky kids...and then have super-tired, miserable children for the rest of the day.

When you do go out, make sure they have drinks, snacks, toys—do whatever you can within reason to ensure they will be happy (and pleasant for others to be around). Especially when they get a little older, explain to them what is about to happen: "When we finish lunch, we are all going to go to Daddy's work for a special grown-ups party. There will be a lot of Daddy's grown-up friends, and it will be extra-important for you to stay quiet and mind Mommy." "After breakfast, we are going to the doctor. She is going to do things like put a special circle on your chest to listen to your heart, use a special flashlight to look in your mouth, and feel your tummy. Mommy will be right there with you, and when we're finished we'll come home and have a snack." Tell them and show them as much as you can to prepare them for unusual outings and events, including what your expectations are for their behavior. You'll be amazed at how much they are able understand, even months before they are able to speak, themselves. If you expect your children to behave well, you have to "set them up for success."

Six Months Old and Interested in the World

One change that I read about and definitely noticed in our girls was a "heightened sense of awareness" at around six months old. Up until that point, we could vacuum under their crib while they were sleeping, play the piano during a nap, or bowl down the hallway if we felt like it, and it didn't seem to disturb them. At about six months, however, that changed. They still did not often wake each other up, but we started to have to keep it down while they were sleeping. If we were out-and-about, they were extremely interested in and stimulated by their surroundings. Babies who would have previously been able to sleep anytime, anywhere, may become more sensitive to changes in environment at about this time and be unable to nap/sleep if not in their own beds.

Once after our girls had reached this point, we went into their bedroom to check on them before we went to sleep that night. One of the girls started moving around, and afraid of being spotted (and having *two* awake babies on our hands), I quickly darted out the door. Stephen was too far into the room to do that, though, so he immediately dropped to the floor and silently low-crawled out of there. Thankfully, we both escaped, undetected. You never know when that military training will come in handy.

Crib Time

I found that "crib time" was an invaluable part of our daily lives from the time that our girls had their own cribs (at about eight months old in our case) until they were about two years old. "Crib time" was a time of day that I put them in their separate cribs with a few toys and books, with the lights on and playtime music playing in the background, and they played on their own. I usually used this time to take a shower, vacuum, or do some other household chore while I knew they were safe in their cribs—which gave me an extra break in the day in addition to nap time. They seemed to really enjoy the change of scenery and getting a respite from someone else getting in their space and trying to take their toys. We had "crib time" almost every day, and they were usually quite happy to play in their cribs for at least 20 minutes—usually for closer to 45. (Differentiating sleep time by having the lights off, sleepy music playing, and no toys in their beds was effective in giving them the message that "crib time" was play time, but nap time and bed time were sleep times.)

The Power of Suggestion

At some point in our girls' infanthood, I stumbled upon an amusing—yet very helpful—phenomenon: The Power of Suggestion. One night, after one or both of our babies had not slept through the night for a few nights and I was feeling pretty worn out, I said to them as I laid them down to sleep, "And please, if you wake up in the middle of the night tonight, go right back to sleep." I was joking, of course, because they were far too young to understand anything I was saying...or so I thought. They both slept through the night that night! My husband and I laughed about how my "pep talk" had helped them stay asleep, but when I playfully tried it again on another occasion, it worked again! There were *multiple* times that this worked. Maybe it was a fluke, maybe it was the power of suggestion, or maybe they really do understand what we're saying long before we can understand them and just need a little reminder from time to time that, if they wake up at night, it's okay not to wake up Mommy, too.

•9•

This & That

Babies and Dogs

On the way to Shreveport from Georgia, I felt the babies move for the first time. It was just a fluttering feeling, and when I put my hand on my tummy, I could feel a little tapping. That was really thrilling! That was a week ago, and since then I've felt them moving a lot more, and Stephen's had a chance to feel them move some, too. I got tickled the other day because I was sitting on the couch and Sugar (our dog) had her head on my tummy. I felt one of the babies tap against her face, and Sugar jerked up, gave me a look that said, "What in the world was that?!" got up off the couch, and walked away. I guess she'd better get used to it!   -July 19, 2007 (17 weeks)

Our first "baby" is a sixty-something-pound boxer named Sugar. I was never an animal person before, but I love her to pieces. When we were choosing which breed to get, we decided on a boxer largely because of the breed's reputation for being wonderful with children. Even so, we wanted to research how to introduce our dog to our babies to avoid a negative experience, if at all possible.

I urge you to consult additional resources on this one. One tip we found especially helpful was to bring home an article of clothing that one of the babies had worn prior to bringing the babies home from the hospital—that way your dog can become familiar with their scent. Do not let the dog do anything other than gently smell it—any type of rambunctious, rough, or potentially dangerous behavior near the baby-scented item must be immediately stopped and strictly disciplined.

Our dog responded with the same curiosity over the scent of our girls' baby clothing as she had to other unfamiliar people-scents: She was curious, but gentle. What really surprised us with Sugar was how she reacted when we brought the girls home. She was in her crate—her happy place—and Stephen brought the girls into the house, strapped into their infant car seat carriers, and set them down close to the crate so Sugar could see and smell them from a safe distance. Unlike anything she had done before—or since, with the exception of being in the car with us in a drive-through car wash— Sugar began to tremble uncontrollably. I don't know if she sensed who/what they were and was overcome with the intensity of knowing that these tiny beings were somehow part of us and yet not. Or if she somehow knew that these things were intruding into her world, and she was about to lose "only child" status forever. Or if she just really liked their baby smell and desperately wanted to lick them all over and mother them herself. We never would have guessed that she'd tremble like that upon meeting them.

Sugar soon settled down, and then we let her get closer and sniff them a little more. She quickly became much more comfortable with them, but we made her earn our trust. Another helpful tip was to initially strictly forbid the dog from entering certain "baby areas" of the house—in the first days Sugar was not allowed in the nursery at all. After that, she was allowed in the girls' room, but she had to keep her distance from the crib. For a time, she was allowed no physical contact with the babies at all, and once she was, it was only under our close supervision. In short, even though we have the sweetest dog you can imagine, we set up strict boundaries between her and our babies, and she slowly had to earn our trust. It was a privilege for the dog to be around the children, and the way she earned that privilege was to prove that we could depend on her behaving calmly and gently around them.

While I was afraid for a while that she'd stupidly step on and crush one of our tiny infants, she never did any such thing. We have tons of precious pictures of her snuggling up to them—while we were closely supervising her—and she was quite handy in (somewhat grossly) lapping up spit-up spills and enjoying the all-you-can-eat buffet around their high chairs when the girls started on solid food. We have no doubt that she would save them from a speeding locomotive or a boogeyman if it ever came down to it. We love our Sugar dog!

Stephen introducing our girls to Sugar. (You may notice the boxes of Christmas decorations in the background, which stayed on the floor for weeks...What a time!)

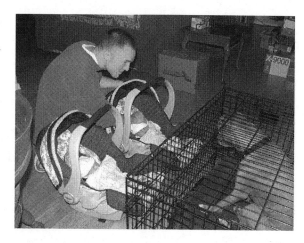

Two for the Road: Traveling with Little Ones

I did not leave the house much for daily errands with our girls while they were infants—it was just too much work, and I had to protect my preemies from the frigid Oklahoma winter and the cold and flu viruses that came with it—but my husband and I quickly found ourselves taking long road trips with them. When our girls were three months old, my husband was assigned to six weeks of Air Force training in Alabama, and so we packed up the minivan (with a TON of baby paraphernalia and our dog in her large crate) and headed to Georgia—home of our parents, three hours away from Stephen's training. While the "15-hour drive" from Oklahoma to Georgia took *forever*, stopping every few hours to nurse two babies, I am glad that we were forced to start traveling with them so early. They slept most of the way on that trip, and have been road-tripping for so much of their lives that our now nine-year-old daughters don't really know to dread a long car trip.

The advantages of traveling with babies: They sleep a lot, and they don't know how to ask, "Are we there yet?" Until our girls became mobile, we drove by day because they slept much of the way. When they began crawling, we decided to drive at night—I felt sorry for them to be strapped into their car seats all day, and I was not about to let my precious babies crawl around on the dirty floor of a restaurant or expose them to the cooties of hotel room carpet. (Yes, I know now that they would have survived, but I couldn't stand the thought of it at the time.) Driving at night was good for the girls, but terrible for us. And after witnessing someone drive the wrong way down the highway at 1:00 in the morning, we swore we would never drive through the night again. Once our girls began walking—and could safely munch on snacks in their car seats—traveling with them became much easier again.

Our second road trip with the girls at six months old
(Photo credit Aunt Allison)

Some things to keep in mind when traveling with little ones:

- Don't try to be in a rush. Trying to hurry will make you crazy, drive your kids crazy, and in the end, you'll still get there at the same, slow pace.
- Those nifty mirrors that strap to the car's seats so you can see their faces while they're in rear-facing car seats are worth the investment.

- Pacifiers with clips will save you having to search the car for tossed/lost pacis.
- Pack the things that are necessary for your children's comfort and familiarity, but don't pack everything you own. Realize that you can bathe babies in a clean kitchen sink if you need to, use regular adult towels instead of hooded baby towels, and so forth.
- Unless you're going to a cabin in the wilderness, you'll probably be fairly close to a Wal-Mart, Walgreens, or Target, where you can find a replacement if you forget to pack something desperately important.
- If you can, have another adult travel with you to reach back and hand them dropped toys, snacks, etc. I have bought a one-way airline ticket for my sister on more than one occasion so she could ride in the car with me and my girls. (She owes me favors—I changed her diapers when she was a baby.) If you travel solo, be sure to put everything within arm's reach: a bag of pre-packaged snacks, a container of DVDs, etc. We tethered toys to our girls' car seats when they were babies so they'd have toys within reach, and when they got older, we started to place a tub of books and toys between their chairs.
- I love the built-in DVD player in our minivan. Our generation survived childhood without such luxuries, but then people used to have surgery without anesthesia, too— why inflict that on our children? Baby Einstein DVDs are a pretty mellow and relatively educational choice for little ones when you need to resort to a back-seat babysitter on the road. Thomas and Friends (trains) DVDs are also pretty peaceful, and our most-recent quiet car ride favorite is Raymond Briggs' The Snowman.
- Favorite non-electronic entertainment for pre-schoolers includes travel-size Magna Doodles; Highlights magazines, Puzzle Buzz, or Hidden Pictures books; Fisher Price View Masters and extra reels; paper dolls; lacing toys; and Crayola dry-erase boards with Crayola (washable!) dry-erase crayons or markers.
- I like to make sure I have some snacks on hand that include protein, in case I need to tide the girls over for a while before

we get to a good place to stop for a meal. Peanut butter crackers and Zbars (by Clif) are two of our favorites. Snack Catchers by Munchkin are nearly spill-proof and are fantastic for holding Cheerios, Goldfish, and other bite-sized fare.

- My "emergency" tub in the back of the van always includes paper towels, baby wipes, toilet paper, and grocery bags.

- Even long after our girls were fully potty-trained, we still traveled with one of their "pink potties" in the car. I just knew that as soon as we left that thing at home, one of them would desperately need to go while we were driving through endless miles of cornfields in the middle of nowhere with no bathroom for miles (hence the emergency toilet paper). When they were first learning to use the potty, we traveled with both pink potties, so that we could lift the tailgate and put them both on a potty at every stop. (I do like to save a few minutes here and there when I can.)

- One of my favorite road trip packing tips: Pack one bathroom bag for the whole family instead of packing each person's toiletries in separate suitcases. We have one big tote bag that holds it all, goes into the bathroom when we arrive, corrals everything so it's either neatly contained out of our host's way in the bathroom, or so we can easily get our bathroom junk out of their bathroom when bath/shower/tooth-brushing time is complete.

- An epiphany from one hotel visit: Instead of lifting the girls up to brush their teeth in the hotel sink (sans step-stool), I told them to lean over the bathtub. It was much easier, and they thought it was fun!

- If you're flying with infants, note that each row of seats only contains one extra oxygen mask, so only one adult with a lap baby can sit in each row. The first time we flew with our girls, we did not know this, the online reservations system did not know this, the gate agents didn't notice this—it wasn't until we were on board that a flight attendant had us scrambling to change seats. We ended up passing books, snacks, and toys up and down the aisle, thanks to some very patient fellow passengers. If traveling with both your babies in your laps, try to book your seats across the aisle from each other or right behind each other for ease of sharing stuff—and if you have a kicker or two, at least one of the people getting kicked in the back will be your spouse, not an innocent stranger.

- Most airlines are great about allowing parents to check baby gear for free. Checked car seats usually require some type of car seat travel bag. Reusable versions of these can be purchased for $10-$100 (search online for "car seat travel bag"). Some airlines will provide a giant plastic bag for this purpose; others offer them for $10 or so at check-in. Car seats and Pack-N-Plays are usually checked free of charge at check-in. Strollers are typically checked at the gate—or at the bottom of the ramp right before you step into the plane—free of charge. Check with your airline before flying to see what their policies are for baby gear.

- Also check with your airline and/or the TSA for the current policies for transporting baby food, full bottles and sippy cups, and breast milk.

- Your greatest challenge if you fly without another adult may be getting from your car into the terminal building with two or more children and all of their gear. If you don't have a kind friend who is willing to take you to the airport, you may choose to park at one of those privately owned offsite airport parking lots. Their shuttle buses pick you up at your parking space, drop you off at the terminal building, and return you directly to your parking spot at the end of your trip. The drivers will almost always help you with your bags. (And I'm sure they appreciate a generous tip!)

- Aside: My husband quickly got comfortable with the idea of tipping extra to compensate for the circus show we were every time we hit the road, especially if we had left a mess behind.

Toy Management

At this point, you know what a Type-A person I am, so keeping toys under control—and still enjoyed—is a challenge for me. We have tried to keep most of the girls' toys in their room, with a few items rotated in-and-out of our living area. This way, they have things to play with out where the action is, but our adult space is not completely overrun with plastic stuff.

When they were babies, I read or heard somewhere that piling all their toys into a deep toy box is no good, because small children play best with their toys when they can easily see them. I happened to have a shallow, clear, plastic under-the-bed container handy, and it became the girls' living room toy box for years thereafter. Every so often, I would swap some living room toys with toys from their bedroom, to keep the selection fresh. They also enjoyed easily climbing in and out of it, themselves! Occasionally, I emptied it on a hot day, put it on our patio, filled it with water, and had a fun, outside splash activity for them that did not necessitate me sitting in a baby pool with two babies.

Potty Training

This is one area in which I claim no expertise. God blessed us with babies who ate well, slept well, were well... Maybe He figured I could handle a curve-ball when the girls were two-and-a-half. While I cannot offer advice on the "right way" to potty train, I will tell you that if I had to do it over again, I would not try to push it. We tried the *Potty Training in Less Than a Day* method, and while that may work for some kids, it was miserable for us. I waited until our girls were showing all the "readiness cues" that you read about in every parenting book and web resource, and I still don't think they were ready. And when one of them resisted, I wish I had chosen not to fight that battle—it became a control issue with her for months thereafter. The pee-pee training was not so bad, but the poop-training took more than a year. And in the end, I think I learned that that's one thing they'll do on their own schedule, and there's nothing you can do about it besides encouraging and rewarding their successes, and being VERY patient.

Big Kid Beds

Ah, Melanie, and her words of wisdom. Another nugget she passed on to me was to wait as long as possible to put our girls in "big girl beds." One of her daughters stayed in her crib until she was three, and the transition was a snap. Her other daughter was too tall for her crib at 18 months, and they had a horrible time getting her to understand that she had to stay in her bed even though she could physically climb out. The older they are, the better they'll be able to understand the new rules that go along with the new beds. Our girls were three, and the rule was that their "big girl beds" were just like their cribs—they were not allowed to get out. They would call Mommy and Daddy first and wait for us to come and get them, or they would be in trouble. It was a very easy transition for us, and I am so thankful we didn't do it any sooner!

Stay-At-Home Mommyhood

Long before we had children, I knew that I wanted to stay home with them, and my husband has always been very supportive of this idea. When I became pregnant, I had already eased out of full-time work: Knowing when we moved to Oklahoma that we were hoping to start a family made it a convenient time for me not to try to get another full-time job and do some private tutoring and volunteer work, instead. For a lot of moms, though, I know the decision is not so simple. And expecting twins instead of "just one" can throw a monkey wrench in whatever plans you may have had before—childcare times two is a different proposition than childcare for one, for starters.

I know some moms who have loved every minute of staying home with their children—or at least that's what they say. Most of us struggle with it from time to time, though. It's exhausting teaching children to become decent human beings, for one thing, and yet at the end of the day, you sometimes can't help thinking to yourself, "What have I accomplished today???" Hopefully, though, you'll be able to remember that raising the next generation is an important endeavor, and while someone else may be able to provide daily care for your children, no one else can do it with the same passionate desire for their best interest that you can.

Of my friends who are stay-at-home moms, those who are most content are those who surround themselves with others who support what they do for a living. My husband is my number one champion, and my extended family is behind me all the way. I have a circle of friends who also stay home with their children—without each other's support and understanding of what daily life is like, there are days that I might lose my mind. I encourage you to seek out relationships with other stay-at-homers—most communities have chapters of Mothers of Preschoolers (www.mops.org) or other similar organizations, which is a great place to start. Chat up other moms at local parks, Kindermusik—wherever you spend time with your children. You'll be glad you did!

If you go back to work outside the home, my advice is the same: Surround yourself with people who understand and support you, your circumstances, and your choices. We all need people! New mommyhood is full of joys and struggles, all of which are so much better borne within a community of love and support.

•Afterword•

It will get easier!

The first year with twins is hard. Sleep deprivation times two is hard. Babies constantly growing and changing times two is hard. Babies crawling in two different directions is cute, but hard. But it does get easier. And it gets really cool.

After the first year, they sleep more, and they sleep more consistently—which means you sleep more. Juggling only one or two naps a day frees you up to get more done both inside and outside of the house. No more bottles; no more breastfeeding. They continue to change, but not at the same rapid, fly-by-the-seat-of-your-pants pace that you experience in the first year, so you get a chance to catch your breath. And they start to really play with each other! When our girls were about two years old, there was a period of time when every day at naptime, they'd talk to each other in their cribs for 45 minutes or so before falling asleep for an hour and a half or more—what a nice chunk of Mommy-time! Our home is the constant stage for their imaginative play, and the games they come up with together are never-ending.

Twins have a life-long best friend to play with all day, every day. Do they fight sometimes? Sure—just as any siblings do. But they're the best of friends again in no time. Seeing them grow up together and interact with each other is fascinating and entertaining in a way that constantly makes you feel that you're witnessing something extraordinary. Our girls have been more of a blessing to us than we could have ever imagined, and what's more, they are an amazing gift from God for each other.

Abigail and Caroline as flower girls, age 2 ½

•Acknowledgements•

"Why did this happen to us???"

Let's face it—in the first few hours and even days after learning we were expecting twins, that was my honest thought: Why is this is happening to us? Not that we were being blessed beyond what my anxious heart could fathom, not that this was happening *for* us, but that it was happening *to* us. Gradually, I began to find peace and see the blessing, even before our girls were born. And after they were born, one look at those sweet babies, even hooked up to every necessary technology, and I knew that God had filled our storehouse to overflowing. To Him, I am so thankful.

For many reasons, without my husband, none of this would have been possible. Thank you, Stephen, for being my best friend, partner in life, daddy to our girls, and my steadfast champion.

Many dear friends and family members have also encouraged me, edited for me, helped me network, made contributions—directly to the writing of this book and in giving us invaluable support and advice as we navigated the first years with our girls: Dr. K, Dr. S, our hospital's fabulous obstetric and NICU nursing staff, Annette, Melanie, Dr. P, Dr. Sonny Castro, Mary Castro, Dr. W, Lindsey, Aimee, Colleen, Ellengray, Julie-Rose, my wonderful parents, Ward and Mary Julia Hiss, and my devoted sister, Allison. Many thanks and love to you all!

•About the Author•

Thank you so much for reading this book! I hope that it is a help to you—even if only in a small way. Our family's Air Force life has made me embrace the idea that even making a small difference for a small time may make an important and long-lasting difference to others. No matter how short a time we spend in a place, I try to live it to the fullest, love people truly (though saying goodbye is always tough), and do whatever I feel called to do for however long we are there. Likewise, it was worth it to me to write this book if it made your first year with twins even a little bit easier.

What was life like before our twins were born? My husband Stephen and I were high school sweethearts, band kids in love in Marietta, Georgia. Though I was set on chasing him to Colorado when he went to the Air Force Academy, my daddy made me see reason—that paying out of state tuition would be ludicrous when I could attend the University of Georgia for free—and a Georgia Bulldog I became. I graduated in early May of 2001 with a Bachelor of Business Administration degree in marketing, and Stephen graduated later that month. Nine days later, we were married and began our life together of "Home is where the Air Force sends us."

About half-way into my business degree, I decided that what I really wanted to do was to become a teacher, but not wanting to slow down my progress toward graduation (and getting married), I finished that degree, determined to earn my teaching credentials later. After a couple of years of substitute teaching as we moved from Georgia to Colorado to Mississippi, we landed in Shreveport, Louisiana, where we stayed long enough for me to complete my Master of Arts in Teaching degree and spend some time teaching second and fifth grades.

When we were getting ready to move to Oklahoma, baby fever hit me, and we decided that I would not pursue a full-time teaching job after our move, hoping that we might be blessed with *a* baby. I worked as a Title-I reading tutor for an elementary school, did some private tutoring, and volunteered with some math students at another school until driving around in our little town became too much for our two babies in utero.

While I've been a full-time stay-at-homer ever since, there always seem to be other things to do. In Missouri, I co-founded Warrensburg Area Mothers of Multiples, a mothers of twins group that was a sweet source of support and friendship in our little community. We enjoyed partnering with the Multiples of Kansas City club and the Missouri Organization of Mothers of Twins Clubs, where we found an even greater network of support. I've enjoyed volunteering at my daughters' schools in various capacities, knowing first-hand how much of a difference it makes to our classroom teachers to have some extra help from time-to-time, and the role of Air Force wife has kept me pretty busy, as well. But oh, the relationships! I love the friends we've made on this journey so far and am so thankful for all of the places that have afforded us the opportunity to love so many so dearly.

Now, what about you? If you'd like to connect, I'd love to get to know you, too!

www.susannastwinsanity.com

Facebook: https://www.facebook.com/susannastwinsanity

Instagram: https://www.instagram.com/susanna1210

Pinterest: https://www.pinterest.com/susanna7

•Appendix•

Keeping Track

I found it very helpful for the first several weeks to have a notebook on the changing table where I kept track of who ate at what time, on what side, who had poopy diapers, and so forth. This was also a good place to make notes if their poop looked weird and for how long—I know that sounds gross and bizarre, but your pediatrician will ask about the quantity and quality of their stools to determine if they're having digestive problems. (For the next several years, you will find yourselves talking about poop more than you ever dreamed possible.)

Nowadays, there are some great apps out there that enable you to do the same thing. Baby Connect has great reviews, allows you to track multiple babies, and it enables users to log-on from different devices—perfect for both mom and dad to use, as well as nursery workers and anyone else whose notes you need to have. Go to http://www.baby-connect.com or the App Store to download.

If you prefer pencil-and-paper, the following pages include sample charts, one filled out as an example and one blank. I usually just kept a notebook and jotted down a chart like this, but you're welcome to print copies of the blank one if you like. After a while, I stopped keeping track of time so much and just noted whether or not they'd pooped and who had eaten first that day.

Date: Thursday, May 26

Name: Razzle

Time	Feeding Side	Feeding Duration	Wet Diaper	Dirty Diaper
7:00 am	L	30 min	X	X
8:30 am			X	X
10:00 am	R	25 min	X	X
11:30 am			X	
1:00 pm	L	20 min	X	
2:30 pm			X	
4:00 pm	R	15 min	X	X
5:30 pm			X	
7:00 pm	L	30 min	X	X
10:00 pm	R	25 min	X	X
1:00 am	L	20 min	X	
4:00 am	R	20 min	X	X

Name: Dazzle

Time	Feeding Side	Feeding Duration	Wet Diaper	Dirty Diaper
7:30 am	R	25 min.	X	X
9:00 am			X	
10:30 am	L	30 min	X	X
12:00 pm			X	
1:25 pm	R	25 min	X	X
3:00 pm			X	
4:30 pm	L	20 min	X	X
6:00 pm			X	
7:25 pm	R	25 min	X	X
10:30 pm	L	25 min	X	X
1:25 am	R	25 min	X	
4:25 am	L	20 min	X	X

Date:

Name:

Time	Feeding Side	Feeding Duration	Wet Diaper	Dirty Diaper

Name:

Time	Feeding Side	Feeding Duration	Wet Diaper	Dirty Diaper

Recommended Resources

Books

Juggling Twins by Meghan Regan-Loomis: I wish this book had been published when I was expecting! Regan-Loomis often had me laughing out loud as I reviewed this book. She and I have different perspectives on many issues, but I would recommend that any parent expecting twins read her book and mine in order to get a wide range of ideas on how to manage life with two babies.

Regan-Loomis, Meghan. Juggling Twins: The Best Tips, Tricks, and Strategies from Pregnancy to the Toddler Years. Naperville: Sourcebooks, Inc., 2008. Print.

On Becoming Baby Wise by Gary Ezzo & Robert Bucknam: A great starting point for getting your babies to sleep.

Ezzo, Gary, and Robert Bucknam. On Becoming Baby Wise: Giving Your Infant the Gift of Nighttime Sleep. Louisiana, Missouri: Parent-Wise Solutions, 2001.

The Mother of All Pregnancy Books, The Mother of All Baby Books, and The Mother of All Toddler Books by Ann Douglas: I much prefer this series to What to Expect, which often had me panicking over what might be going wrong with my pregnancy or my babies. The Mother of All books are comprehensive, yet still warmly written and pleasant to read.

Douglas, Ann. The Mother of All Baby Books. New York: Wiley Publishing, Inc., 2002.

The Happiest Baby on the Block by Harvey Karp: In this book, Dr. Karp asserts that the first three months of babies' lives are to be treated much as a fourth trimester of pregnancy. He strongly advocates swaddling to simulate life inside the womb, and he offers remedies for helping colicky babies.

Karp, Harvey. The Happiest Baby on the Block. New York: Random House Publishing Group, 2003.

Your Baby & Child by Penelope Leach: This is the book that my mother read when I was a baby, and then she passed it on to me. The information is mostly timeless, and yet the writing does take you back to the 1970s. Leach's British-isms also amused me, as when she says, "You can make your baby perfectly clean by 'topping and tailing,'" which loosely translates in the American vernacular to washing your baby's face and backside. If you want to check out the lovingly-written guide that your mother likely used, look for this one.

Leach, Penelope. Your Baby & Child: From Birth to Age Five. New York: Alfred A. Knopf, Inc., 1978.

Websites

ABCs of Breastfeeding from the Stanford School of Medicine: This site offers excellent details and photographs on how to breastfeed. http://newborns.stanford.edu/Breastfeeding/ABCs.html

Barbara Luke Maternity: This site not only sells maternity wear specially designed for expectant moms of multiples, but offers pregnancy resources from Dr. Luke, as well. http://www.drbarbaraluke.com/

Breastfeeding.com: This site boasts the "largest directory of lactation consultants anywhere": http://www.breastfeeding.com

BreastFeedingPlace.com: You'll find all kinds if practical, helpful information about breastfeeding, and they even have a page devoted to nursing multiples. http://www.breastfeedingplace.com/

Car Seats for the Littles: Staffed by nationally certified Child Passenger Safety Technicians, this blog provides thorough reviews of car seats, as well as a convenient tool for comparing multiple makes and models. http://csftl.org/

The International Lactation Consultant Association: http://www.ilca.org

La Leche League: Another great resource for breastfeeding, this site can also help you locate a local lactation consultant if you need some in-person assistance. http://www.llli.org/

Mayo Clinic: Obviously a great resource for all things medical, but also a good place to look for answers to questions like, "Should I allow my babies to use pacifiers?" and "How should I take my baby's temperature?" www.mayoclinic.org

Multiples of America: Formerly known as The National Organization of Mothers of Twins Clubs, this site can not only help you locate the multiples club nearest you, but also has a wealth of resources for parents of twins and higher-order multiples. http://www.multiplesofamerica.org/

NICUawareness.org: Find resources and support on how to be involved in your babies' care in the NICU, feeding them in the NICU, and what to expect and how to manage life when you take your preemies home. http://www.nicuawareness.org/

SeatCheck.org: Visit this site to find a child safety seat inspection location near you, as well as up-to-date information on safety seat recalls, child passenger safety laws, and other safety tips. www.seatcheck.org

Sidelines National High Risk Pregnancy Support Network: A great support site for women experiencing high risk pregnancies, especially for those on bed rest. www.sidelines.org

TakeThemAMeal.com: Excellent tool for organizing meals. Share this address with a close friend who can round up people to provide meals for your family after the babies are born. It even has a "Click here to order" link for people who want to send a meal to you without actually cooking anything. http://takethemameal.com/

Timeline of a Breastfed Baby: This blog offers lots of great details about what to expect in the first days nursing, plus expectations for breastfeeding moms and their babies at monthly milestones through the first year. http://www.thealphaparent.com/2011/12/timeline-of-breastfed-baby.html

Twiniversity: This blog is full of "Community, Knowledge, Humor," just as its tagline boasts. One of the best resources on this site is its electronic magazine, "Multiplicity." http://www.twiniversity.com/

Other Moms

Multiples of America: Again, check their website to find a mothers of twins club near you. Meeting and talking with other parents of multiples can be a great support, both before and after your babies are born. http://www.multiplesofamerica.org/

Mothers of Preschoolers: Most communities have at least one chapter of MOPS International. They typically meet about twice a month and offer both social and educational programs, as well as childcare during meetings. Adult conversation is invaluable for parents of little ones! See their website to find a club near you. http://www.mops.org/

Recipes to Make Ahead and Freeze

Tips for Freezing & Reheating:

- Freeze soups in single-serving containers for faster thawing and re-heating. It also makes it easy to heat up as few or as many servings as you choose.
- If you're going to heat up several soup servings, place frozen soup in a crock pot on low in the morning, and you'll have hot soup in time for dinner.
- If you want to assemble a casserole and freeze the whole thing before cooking, line your casserole dish with aluminum foil. Once it hardens in the freezer, you can pop it out of the casserole dish (so you don't have your dish held hostage in the freezer), and wrap the frozen casserole in extra foil. When you're ready to cook it, remove the extra foil, and pop it back into the original casserole dish to thaw and cook.
- I like to freeze cooked casseroles in single servings, wrapped in foil, and placed in a large zip-top baggie. That way, I can easily heat up as few or as many servings as I choose.
- Label everything with contents and date. We like to keep a notepad on top of the deep freezer so we know what's hidden in there without having to dig.

Chicken & Dumplings
Dolly McSwain

- 4 boneless, skinless chicken breasts
- 5 cans of chicken broth
- salt and pepper to taste
- 1 medium onion, chopped
- 2 bunches green onions, chopped
- 1 stick butter
- 4 c. milk
- 2 x 8 oz. cans biscuits

In a large pot, boil chicken in chicken broth for 45 minutes. Add onion, green onions, salt and pepper, butter, and milk. Simmer on medium heat for 45 minutes. Pinch each biscuit into small pieces and slowly drop into mixture, stirring constantly. Simmer another 30-45 minutes on medium heat until biscuits are done, stirring occasionally.

Chicken Pockets

- 3 oz. cream cheese, softened
- 3 T butter or margarine, softened, divided
- 2 c. cubed cooked chicken*
- 2 T milk
- ¼ tsp. salt*
- 1/8 tsp. black pepper
- 1 T chopped chives or green onions
- 1 T chopped green bell pepper
- 1 T chopped pimiento
- 1 8 oz. can refrigerated crescent rolls or crescent sheets
- ¾ c. crushed seasoned croutons

*10 oz. canned chicken can be substituted. If you used canned chicken, do not add salt.

Preheat oven to 350°. Blend cream cheese and 2 T butter. Add all other filling ingredients, mixing well. Separate crescent rolls into 4 squares, pressing to seal perforations. Spoon equal amounts of filling into center of each square. Pull corners to center of each square and press to seal. Melt 1 T butter, brush tops of pastry with butter, and top with crushed croutons. Bake on an un-greased cookie sheet 20-25 min. Chicken pockets can be assembled and frozen—extend baking time slightly. Generously serves 2—sparingly serves 4.

Chicken Spaghetti
Melanie H. Griffith

Fills 2 13x9" casserole dishes—cut recipe in half to make 1 casserole dish

- 1 stick of butter
- 8 oz. sour cream
- 1 can cream of mushroom soup
- 1 can cream of chicken soup
- 8 oz. Velveeta cheese
- 8 oz. heavy whipping cream
- black pepper to taste
- 6-8 chicken breast halves, cooked OR meat from 1 rotisserie chicken
- 22-24 oz. uncooked spaghetti

Preheat oven to 350°. Grease 2 13x9" casserole dishes.
Cook spaghetti and set aside.
Cook chicken and cut up into bite-sized pieces and set aside.
In a large, microwaveable bowl, cube the Velveeta and butter, and melt in the microwave (20 seconds, stir, 20 seconds, stir...) Then add soups, sour cream, and pepper, and mix well. Add the cream and chicken and mix well.
Put half of cooked spaghetti in one casserole dish, and half in the other. Pour chicken mixture evenly over spaghetti in both dishes. Bake uncovered at 350° for 20 minutes or until bubbly.

Crock Pot Chicken Tortilla Soup

- 1 packet enchilada sauce mix (or mild taco seasoning mix)
- 1 ½ c. water
- 1 (8 oz.) can tomato sauce
- 1 can cream of chicken soup
- 2 c. milk
- 3-4 boneless, skinless chicken breast halves
- 1 can black beans, drained
- 1 can corn, drained
- 1 (14.5 oz.) can diced tomatoes (southwest style, or petite diced tomatoes with sweet onion, or mild Ro-Tel)

In crock pot, mix the enchilada packet together with the water and tomato sauce. Add cream of chicken soup and milk and whisk together until smooth. Add chicken. Pour drained black beans, drained corn and diced tomatoes on top. Cover and cook on low 6-8 hours. Before serving, take out chicken and shred or dice, then put back and stir it all together. Serve with sour cream, shredded cheddar cheese, lime, avocado, and/or tortilla chips.

Lasagna
Susanna Pippel

- 2 T. olive oil
- ½ c. chopped onion
- 2 cloves garlic, pressed or finely minced
- 1 lb. ground beef
- ½ lb. bulk pork sausage
- 3 c. spaghetti sauce (about 1 regular jar)
- 1 ½ c. water
- 15 oz. cottage cheese
- 2 c. Italian shredded cheese blend
- 1 c. shredded mozzarella or Monterey jack
- ½ c. grated Parmesan cheese
- 2 eggs
- ¼ c. chopped fresh parsley

- ½ tsp. salt
- ¼ tsp. ground black pepper
- 8 oz. lasagna noodles, uncooked

Preheat oven to 350°. Grease 13x9-inch baking dish.

In a large saucepan, sauté onion in olive oil until onion is translucent. Add garlic for just a few seconds (do not let turn brown) before adding ground beef and sausage, and cook until no longer pink; drain. Add spaghetti sauce and water*, and simmer about 10 minutes.
Meanwhile, in a separate bowl, stir together cottage cheese, Italian cheese, Parmesan, eggs, parsley, salt, and pepper.

Cover the bottom of the baking dish in a layer of sauce.
Arrange 3 uncooked noodles over the sauce and top with another layer of sauce.
Cover with ½ cheese filling.
Add a layer of noodles, a layer of sauce, and the other ½ of cheese filling.
Top with another layer of noodles, the remaining sauce, and mozzarella or Monterey jack cheese.

Cover tightly with aluminum foil and bake for 45 min.
Uncover and bake an additional 15 min.
Let stand 10 min. before serving.

*Pour water into empty spaghetti sauce jar and shake before pouring into pan to make sure no sauce is left in the jar.

Sour Cream Chicken Enchiladas
Susanna's Daddy, Ward Hiss

- 4 boneless, skinless chicken breast halves, seasoned to taste (salt, pepper, paprika, garlic powder—whatever!) and cooked OR meat from 1 rotisserie chicken
- ½ c. chicken broth
- 16 oz. sour cream

- 1 can cream of chicken soup
- 1 can chopped green chilies
- 8 oz. shredded Monterey jack cheese
- ½ c. diced onion—you may want to sauté the onions to create a milder flavor
- flour tortillas (8-10 large)
- 1 c. shredded cheddar cheese
- sliced black olives

For serving:
- Shredded lettuce
- Salsa

Preheat oven to 375°. Grease a 13x9" casserole dish.

Cook chicken breasts until tender, being careful not to overcook. Set aside.

Combine chicken broth, sour cream, cream of chicken soup, chilies, Monterey jack cheese, and onion. Reserve 1/3 of sour cream mixture and set aside.

Cut cooked chicken into bite-sized pieces and add to remaining 2/3 of sour cream mixture.

Spoon chicken and sour cream mixture onto flour tortillas, roll up, and arrange in greased casserole dish.

Spoon remaining 1/3 sour cream mixture over enchiladas, and top with cheddar cheese and olives.

Cover tightly and bake at 375° for 45 minutes or until bubbly.

Serve with shredded lettuce and salsa.

Taco Soup

- 2 lbs. ground beef
- 1 large onion, diced
- 1 pkg. taco seasoning
- 1 pkg. ranch style dressing mix
- 1 can diced tomatoes
- 1 can Ro-Tel tomatoes and chilies
- 2 cans pinto beans

- 1 can corn
- 1 can tomato sauce

For serving:
Tortilla chips
Shredded cheddar cheese

Brown ground beef and onion together in a large pot, and then drain. Add remaining ingredients, including all liquids. Simmer on low heat for 30 min. Can be served with tortilla chips and shredded cheese. Makes ~ 12 servings.

Crock Pot Tomato-Basil Parmesan Soup
Karen Petersen of www.365daysofcrockpot.com

- 2 (14 oz) cans diced tomatoes, with juice
- 1 c. finely diced celery
- 1 c. finely diced carrots
- 1 c. finely diced onions
- 1 tsp. dried oregano or 1 T fresh oregano
- 1 T dried basil or 1/4 c. fresh basil
- 4 c. chicken broth
- ½ bay leaf
- ½ cup flour
- 1 c. Parmesan cheese
- ½ c. (1 stick) butter
- 2 c. half and half, warmed
- 1 tsp. salt
- ¼ tsp. black pepper

Add tomatoes, celery, carrots, chicken broth, onions, oregano, basil and bay leaf to crock pot. Cover and cook on LOW for 5-7 hours, until flavors are blended and vegetables are soft. (For a smoother texture, puree this mixture with a stick blender or in batches in a food processor before completing the next steps.)

About an hour before serving prepare a roux: Melt butter over low heat in a saucepan and add flour. Stir constantly with a whisk for

5-7 minutes, until golden but not brown. Slowly stir in 1 cup hot soup. Add another 3 cups and stir until smooth. Add all back into the slow cooker. Stir and add the Parmesan cheese, warmed half and half, salt and pepper. Cover and cook on LOW for another hour until ready to serve.

Makes about 2 quarts

White Chili

- 1 T. olive oil
- 1 lb. boneless skinless chicken breast, cubed
- 1 medium onion, chopped
- 1 can chicken broth
- 4 oz. can chopped green chilies (or ½ freshly cooked chilies)
- 1 clove garlic, minced
- ½ tsp. dried oregano
- ½ tsp. dried parsley
- 1 can pinto beans with liquid

For serving:
- Rice
- Monterey jack cheese
- Green onions

Heat oil in a large pot. Sauté onion and chicken until chicken is browned. Add chicken broth, chilies, and seasonings. Simmer covered for 30 minutes. Add pinto beans with liquid and simmer another 10 minutes. Serve over cooked rice. Garnish with shredded cheese and chopped green onions.

•Index•

apps, 145

baby carriers, 124

baby monitors, 44-45

bassinets, 35

bed rest, 63, 150

big kid beds, 136

birth plan, 61

blankets, 43

bouncy seats, 36

Braxton Hicks contractions, 62

breast pump, 43, 74, 105

breastfeeding, 79
  benefits, 80-81
  breast milk fortifier, 74
  breast pump, 43, 74, 105
  burping, 89
  how to, 82
  how to manage two, 85
  keeping track, 87, 145
  lactation consultant, 74, 82
  milk production, 81
  nipple confustion, 88
  nursing bras, 55
  nursing pillow, 86
  nutrition, 91
  paraphernalia, 44
  storing breast milk, 89
  suck-swallow reflex, 74, 83

burping, 89

car seats, 30, 149-150

Celestone, 65

changing table, 35

classes, 23

clothing, 37

colic, 112, 148

contraction monitor, 64

crib bumpers, 42

crib time, 126

crib(s), 33

c-section, 15, 70

delivery, 70

diapers, 28
  brands, 29
  diaper pails, 30
  how many, 29
  sizes, 28

dogs, 129

fetal heart monitors, 64

fraternal twins, 11

furniture, 33

grocery shopping with babies, 124

helping hands, 20

high risk, 12

human chorionic gonadotropin (hCG), 14

identical twins, 12

keeping track, 87, 145

labor, 64

lactation consultant, 74, 82, 149

laundry, 39

lung development, 65

magnesium sulfate, 65

maternity clothes, 51, 53, 149
  belly band, 54
  bras, 55
  nursing bras, 55
  sizes, 54
  tummy sleeve, 54

membrane, 14

multiples clubs, 19, 51, 151

neonatal intensive care unit (NICU), 72, 75, 150

non-stress tests, 64

pacifiers, 40

perinatal specialist, 12

portable play yards (Pack-n-Plays), 35

potty training, 136

premature labor, 62

recipes, 91, 151

registering for gifts, 24

resources, 148
  books, 148
  other moms, 151
  websites, 149

rocking chair, 35

shopping, 27
  lists, 47
  where to shop, 51

sick baby kit, 41

SIDS, 33, 40, 42

sleep
  giving up naps, 114
  putting babies to sleep, 105
  skipping naps, 114, 125
  through the night, 107
  waking each other up, 104

sleep schedules, 95
  newborn to two months, 103
  two to four months, 106
  four to eight months, 107
  nine to twelve months, 109
  one year and beyond, 111
  toddler years, 111
  when the going gets tough, 112

solid foods, 36, 117

strollers, 32, 123-124

suck-swallow reflex, 74, 83

swings, 36

traveling, 131

twin-to-twin transfusion syndrome (TTTS), 60

wipes, 30

Made in the USA
San Bernardino, CA
11 May 2017